Human Rights Indicators in Development

An Introduction

Siobhán McInerney-Lankford
Hans-Otto Sano

THE WORLD BANK
Washington, D.C.

ISBN: 978-0-8213-8604-0
eISBN: 978-0-8213-8576-0   DOI: 10.1596/978-0-8213-8604-0

Library of Congress Cataloging-in-Publication Data

McInerney-Lankford, Siobhán Alice, 1974–
Human rights indicators in development : an introduction / Siobhán McInerney-Lankford and Hans-Otto Sano.
    p. cm.
  ISBN 978-0-8213-8604-0
  1. Human rights.   2. Economic development.   I. Sano, H.-O. (Hans-Otto)   II. World Bank.
III. Title.
  JC571.M28 2010
  323--dc22

                                                                    2010038085

Contents

List of Tables

List of Figures

List of Boxes

Foreword

The World Bank Study *Human Rights Indicators in Development: An Introduction* offers a preliminary perspective on the relevance of human rights indicators to development practice. It elucidates in general terms the significance of human rights indicators for development processes and outcomes, in particular through how they connect the normative standards embodied in human rights and development data. This study effectively outlines the assessment and diagnostic functions of human rights indicators in the context of development, offering a review of methodological approaches on human rights measurement, exploring in general terms different types of human rights indicators and their potential implications for development at three different levels of convergence or integration. The study also includes a basic conceptual framework for approaching the relationship between rights and development and approaches to human rights integration in development. The study contributes a worthwhile theoretic introduction to a complex issue of growing relevance in a number of areas of development which may be of interest to practitioners and scholars in a variety of institutional settings, including that of the WBG.

Human Rights Indicators in Development: An Introduction is one recent output of broader World Bank Group efforts underway to explore the relevance of human rights to its work. The World Bank contributes to the realization of human rights in different areas and in different ways, whether through improving poor people's access to health, education, food and water, promoting the participation of indigenous peoples in decision-making and or promoting accountability, transparency and governance.

Most recently, the World Bank Group established a knowledge and learning program supported by the Nordic Trust Fund (NTF). The program comprises a range of research, analytical and operational activities across the World Bank Group designed to help the World Bank develop a more informed view on human rights. It is aimed at improving existing Bank involvement on human rights in the overall context of the Bank's core mission of promoting economic growth and poverty reduction. OPCS and LEG are pleased to support the publication of this Study as part of that program and are grateful to the Danish government for the generous support of the research upon which it is founded.

Hassane Cisse,
Deputy General Counsel,
Knowledge and Research,
Legal Vice Presidency,
The World Bank

Abstract

Human rights indicators are central to the application of human rights standards in context and relate essentially to measuring human rights realization, both qualitatively and quantitatively. They offer an empirical or evidence-based dimension to the normative content of human rights legal obligations and provide a means of connecting those obligations with empirical data and evidence and, in this way, relate to human rights accountability and the enforcement of human rights obligations. Human rights indicators are important for both assessment and diagnostic purposes: the assessment function of human rights indicators relates to their use in monitoring accountability, effectiveness, and impact; the diagnostic purpose relates to measuring the current state of human rights implementation and enjoyment in a given context, whether regional, country-specific, or local.

This paper offers a preliminary review of the foregoing in the development context and a general perspective on the significance of human rights indicators for development processes and outcomes. It is not intended to be prescriptive and does not provide specific operational recommendations on the use of human rights indicators in development projects. Nor does it advocate a particular approach or mode of integrating human rights in development or argue for a rights-based approach to development.

This paper is designed to provide development practitioners with a preliminary view on the possible relevance, design, and use of human rights indicators in development policy and practice. It also introduces a basic conceptual framework about the relationship between rights and development, including in the World Bank context. It then moves to methodological approaches on human rights measurement, exploring in general terms different types of human rights indicators and their potential implications for development at three levels of convergence or integration. The paper therefore offers a theoretical introduction to a complex area of growing relevance in a number of areas of development that may be of interest to practitioners and scholars in a variety of institutional settings.

UDHR	Universal Declaration of Human Rights
U.N.	United Nations
UNDP	United Nations Development Programme
UNGC	United Nations Global Compact
UNPO	The Unrepresented Nations and Peoples Organization
WDR	World Development Report
WHOSIS	World Health Organization Statistical Information System

CHAPTER 1

Introduction

Human rights indicators are inextricably linked with the application of human rights standards in context, offering an empirical or evidence-based dimension to the normative content of human rights legal obligations. They are essentially concerned with measuring human rights realization, both qualitatively and quantitatively, and assessing validity from a human rights perspective: in this way, they relate to the core of the methodological challenge that human rights present. That methodological challenge is all the more accentuated in the development context, where the place and role of human rights is still debated and where their instrumental role is still contested.

At another level, human rights indicators relate to human rights accountability and the enforcement of human rights obligations. Human rights indicators are an essential part of monitoring the realization of human rights and about substantiating the legal commitments of states under human rights treaties. They are therefore essential to upholding human rights law obligations and giving definition to the standards at the heart of human rights law. As a result, human rights indicators relate also to assessing empowerment and, in the development context, the empowerment of the poorest and most vulnerable rights-holders and those with least access to public goods and services or to channels of political participation.

Finally, there is, in the broader human rights community, a growing interest in clarifying the function and potential of human rights indicators, for both assessment and diagnostic purposes. The assessment function of human rights indicators relates to their use in assessing accountability, effectiveness, and impact; the diagnostic purpose relates to measuring the current state of human rights implementation and enjoyment in a given context, whether regional, country-specific, or local.

This is an introductory paper about the relevance of human rights to the development context and the use of human rights indicators in development activities. It is designed to provide development practitioners with some preliminary perspectives on the relevance, design, and use of human rights indicators in development policy and practice. It explores some of the conceptual challenges confronted in working with human rights indicators and offers a methodological perspective on possible ways to integrate human rights into development policies and programming. It also offers some theoretical perspectives on development and human rights more generally and includes an introduction to the U.N. human rights treaty framework and the work on indicators being developed under that. The paper begins with a basic conceptual perspective on the relationship between human rights and development and moves to methodological approaches on human rights measurement based on different levels and types of integration or convergence. It therefore offers a basic introduction and initial theoretical foundation for the possible formulation of operational approaches to human rights in development projects.

It is important to note, however, that this paper is not intended to be prescriptive and does not provide specific operational recommendations on the use of human rights indicators in development projects. Nor does it advocate a particular approach or mode of integrating human rights in development or argue for a rights-based approach to development. Both the adoption of a human rights–based approach and the integration of human rights are distinct from the definition and use of human rights indicators, although, as this review illustrates, some reliance on human rights indicators is implied whatever the mode or approach taken to human rights integration.

CHAPTER 2

Human Rights and Development: Toward Mutual Reinforcement

Introduction

This chapter offers some perspectives about human rights and development to frame the ensuing discussion of their interrelationship and the role of human rights indicators. "Human Rights [. . .] are literally the rights that one has because one is human."[1] A human right is "a universal moral right, something which all men everywhere, at all times ought to have, something of which no one may be deprived without a grave affront to justice, something which is owing to every human being simply because he is human."[2] The organizing principles and legal standards relied upon in this introduction are those of international human rights law. The relevant sources of international human rights obligation are customary international law, *jus cogens* or obligations *erga omnes*,[3] general international law,[4] and the treaties that comprise the international human rights treaty framework. At the heart of the latter is the "international bill of rights," which is the foundation of the modern international human rights law, comprising the Universal Declaration on Human Rights (1947)[5] and two covenants: the ICCPR and the ICESCR (1966). In addition to these instruments, there are seven core international treaties, which cover racism, discrimination against women, torture, the rights of the child, the rights of migrant workers and their families, the rights of persons with disabilities, and enforced disappearances (not yet enforced). Each treaty establishes a committee of experts to monitor the implementation of treaty provisions by state parties. Some of these treaties are supplemented by optional protocols that address additional concerns or provide a means for individuals to send individual communications alleging violations of particular treaty rights.[6]

The operative understanding of human rights relied on in this paper is derived from the international human rights law framework comprised of these core treaties. This framework is of pervasive relevance to this paper, through its broad substantive coverage and the obligations it generates that are applicable to several areas and at separate levels (dimensions, principles, obligations) and supported by institutions and processes that have developed a well-established body of jurisprudence over many years.[7] Beyond these treaties in force, however, the international human rights law framework continues to evolve, through the ratification of new human rights instruments, the establishment of new international courts and tribunals adjudicating human rights law issues, and the increasing understanding of the relevance of human rights to new areas, such as corporate social responsibility, corporate actors, international organizations, and the fields of environment, trade, intellectual property, and development. This report is primarily concerned with the last of these, and, for its part too, development has evolved considerably. The current understanding of the concept of development is broad-based and multifaceted,[8] emphasizing social and human in addition to economic development. The breadth of perspectives that underpin development today is evident in the Millennium Goals, in which poverty reduction goals are expressed in terms of incomes but also social and environmental change and in relation to gender.[9] The *Millennium Report* likewise evidences an expansive understanding of development, its proper remit, and its objectives. In the World Bank, this more holistic conception was reflected in the Comprehensive Development Framework[10] and evident in its tackling issues such as discrimination, health epidemics, state fragility, post-conflict situations, as well as a host of governance and institutional questions, including corruption. Similar breadth is evident in the World Bank *Social Development Strategy* (2004), which is founded on the principles of cohesion, inclusion, and accountability.[11] The WDR 2006 on *Equity and Development* offered clear endorsement of a broadened understanding of development and to the place of equity in development strategies. U.N. agencies such as the UNDP build policies on a similarly comprehensive conceptualization of development, highlighting human freedom, choice, and participation.[12] A consensus has therefore emerged on the need for a holistic approach to development, but the question of whether and how to integrate human rights in that understanding is still debated. Some argue that the goals of development can and should be formulated in human rights terms,[13] whereas others contend that the relationship is better understood as a process of convergence, the end result of which is not yet settled as far as development strategies are concerned.

The debate about human rights in development and human rights–based approaches to development has gained prominence over the past 10 years as a result of an evolution in thinking in both areas and a reevaluation of development programs since the Vienna World Conference on Human Rights in 1993. The Secretary-General's 2002 Report *In Larger Freedom*, submitted in advance of the Millennium Review Summit, gave strong endorsement to the links between development and human rights.[14] Certain strands of the debate have resulted in a bridging of gaps between development and human rights. Comparing current debates and discourse with those of the late 1990s, a number of changes can be observed. First, there has been a growing acceptance of the place of economic and social rights in development policy;[15] stronger donor focus on empowerment and equity have made social rights fulfilment a more consistent priority. Second, there is a more prevalent integration of human rights and governance policy of donors and international organizations, i.e., the governance agenda of donors has been broadened to encompass human rights. Third, there is a more prominent and substantiated linkage of human rights, development, and security, as well as state fragility, as exemplified in the U.N. Secretary-General's Report *In Larger Freedom*. Fourth, an understanding has emerged of the connection between human rights and environmental and energy development, including questions related to environmental justice[16] and climate change.[17] Notwithstanding such changes, obstacles to the integration of human rights in development remain. The fact that the Millennium Development Goals were formulated without reference to human rights is illustrative of the challenges.[18] Reviewing how the MDGs affect human rights and development integration, Philip Alston observed that the "acknowledgement of the importance of human rights [in development policy] has yet to have a systematic impact on the ground."[19]

However, recent developments support a growing convergence between development and human rights, identifying synergies and commonalities and highlighting the mutual relevance of the two spheres rather than the disconnects or tensions between them.[20] This is consistent with a growing trend among donors toward integrating human rights into development strategies, ranging from full human rights–based approaches, to human rights mainstreaming, human rights dialogues, specific human rights projects, and the implicit or nonexplicit incorporation of human rights considerations.[21] Commentators have taken as their starting points for complementary strategies the overlapping spheres of influence and the interdependence of issues. The emergence of increasingly more holistic conceptions of development is consistent with this, offering an opportunity for identifying common overall objectives and "mutual reinforcement."[22] It is now widely viewed that human rights have relevance for other international goals, including development. The 2003 *U.N. Common Understanding on a Human Rights–Based Approach to Development Cooperation* (Stamford Declaration)[23] and the 2005 *U.N. Millennium*

Project Report evidence this. So too did the Secretary General's 2005 report *In Larger Freedom*, predicated on the connection of human rights to sustainable development and security. Human rights have been central to the U.N. reform agenda, as evidenced in "Action 2" and the interagency Plan of Action (2004–2008), which placed a strong emphasis on mainstreaming and on support to country-level efforts of Member States. In 2008, the Secretary General issued a Policy Decision on Human Rights and Development prompting the establishment of a new UNDG mechanism on human rights mainstreaming to promote a coordinated and coherent U.N. system-wide approach toward the integration of human rights principles and international standards into U.N. operational activities for development.

Under the aegis of the OECD Development Assistance Committee (DAC) Network on Governance (Govnet) Human Rights Task Team,[24] a study was commissioned entitled *Integrating Human Rights in Development: A Synthesis of Donor Approaches and Experiences,* 2006. That work outlines in broad terms the various ways in which development practice had developed to embrace human rights considerations and the varied levels at which integration can take place and the different forms it can assume. The study formed the basis of an "Action-Oriented Policy Paper on Human Rights and Development" that was approved by the OECD DAC in February 2007. The paper includes 10 principles to guide the process of integrating human rights into development.[25] The work of the task team has continued to explore the connections between human rights and development in a number of substantive areas, including aid effectiveness, the connections and mutual relevance of the Paris Declaration Principles and human rights,[26] the nexus between human rights and state fragility, and conflict prevention, and the link between human rights and pro-poor growth. Finally, relevant connections between human rights and development are strongly manifest in the European Union's (EU) approach to human rights in its external relations and increasingly in its approach to development cooperation, including in its 2001 Guidelines on Human Rights Dialogues and in the 2006 Council Regulation establishing a European Instrument on Human Rights and Democratisation.[27]

World Bank Approach to Convergence

The World Bank's approach to human rights can be characterized as broadly supportive of human rights discourse without being explicitly, systematically, or strategically engaged in it.[28] Since the late 1990s, the Bank has posited its role as supporting the realization of human rights.[29] Although some of its public statements have emphasized economic and social rights more than civil and political rights,[30] others have underscored the indirect benefits of its activities on a broader range of human rights.[31] Marking the 50th anniversary of the Universal Declaration of Human Rights, the Bank issued a publication entitled *Development and Human Rights: The Role of the World Bank* (1998).[32] It states:

> The Bank contributes directly to the fulfilment of many human rights articulated in the Universal Declaration. Through its support of primary education, health care and nutrition, sanitation, housing and the environment, the Bank has helped hundreds of millions of people attain crucial economic and social rights. In other areas, the Bank's contributions are necessarily less direct, but perhaps equally significant. By helping to fight corruption, improve transparency and accountability in governance, strengthening judicial systems and modernizing financial sectors, the Bank contributes to building environments in which people are better able to pursue a broader range of human rights.[33]

The 2006 World Development Report on *Equity and Development* explored the ways in which structural and distributional inequalities can hinder development. The overall policy implication of the report, as well as its substantive messages about inequities within and between countries, are consistent with a number of key human rights principles. More recently, the Bank launched the Nordic Trust Fund, an initiative designed to develop a more informed view among Bank staff on how human rights relate to the Bank's core work and mission of promoting economic growth and poverty reduction. "The NTF is a $20 million multi-year and multi donor internal knowledge and learning program which will support activities that capture and make available knowledge about how human rights relate to the Bank's analytical sector/thematic work, including strategy, planning and implementation and, increase awareness among staff and management of how the Bank's work and human rights are related and how human rights aspects can be applied to the Bank's work."[34]

Although not reflective of an official World Bank approach, successive General Counsels of the World Bank have emphasized the positive linkages between human rights and development practices, offering increasingly explicit endorsement of human rights as relevant to standard-setting in development and conducive of accountability and empowerment. As General Counsel between 2003 and 2006, Roberto Dañino stated that "all human rights are indivisible, interdependent and interrelated" and in asserting his view of the relevance of both types of rights to the Bank, set forth a new perspective on the political prohibitions of the Articles.[35] Later, Roberto Dañino wrote: "The significance of this for the Bank is that, in my opinion, it can and should take into account human rights because, given the way international law has evolved with respect to concepts of sovereignty and interference, the Bank would not fall foul of the political prohibitions of the Articles. Globalization has forced us to broaden the range of issues that are of global concern. Human rights lie at the heart of that global challenge."[36] In 2006, the then World Bank Group General Counsel, Ana Palacio, characterized the relevance of human rights in the following terms: "Human rights now constitute defined legal standards of the international constitutional order. Seven core international human rights treaties have been ratified by the majority of the world's countries. A significant body of international legal obligations and jurisprudence now exists with respect to a core of civil and political as well as economic, social and cultural rights"[37] These statements offer a view of an evolving and increasingly permissive view of the Bank's Articles of Agreement relative to human rights. They locate human rights *within* the broad legal framework of the Articles, outlining the seminal influence of international law on the evolution of the Articles' interpretation.

Notwithstanding the foregoing, the official approach of the Bank is based on outlining the substantive and factual ways in which its activities overlap with the human rights through the reach of Bank projects and program areas touching upon human rights.[38] This is confirmed also in the orientation of the new Nordic Trust Fund and its principal aim of increasing awareness among staff and management of how the Bank's work and human rights are related and how human rights aspects can be applied to the Bank's work. In this way, the approach acknowledges the substantive interrelatedness of human rights and development but remains nonexplicit in terms of the direct or formal relevance of specific duties or international treaty obligations. In assessing the relevance of human rights indicators for development, it is therefore important to recognize the legal and institutional constraints within which several international development institutions, including most multilateral development banks, still operate. In the case of the World Bank, it is apposite to note the special relevance of the political prohibitions emanating from Articles III, Section 10, and IV, Section 10, of the IBRD Articles of Agreement.[39] These considerations provide the backdrop for any appraisal of the integration of human rights in the policies and programs of those institutions and remain strongly determinative of the potential for the relevance of human rights indicators in practice. The appropriate response to such inquiries in particular institutional contexts warrants in-depth research and careful individual consideration and lies beyond the scope of this paper.

Role of Human Rights in Development

Beyond factual observations related to convergence lies the question of the value that human rights offer development and the roles they may play in this context. Human rights and development have experienced a form of "rapprochement" in recent years, and this part of the discussion considers reasons for this and bases for the integration of human rights in development and the value-added of human rights in this context.

1. Figure 1.1 illustrates the potential role of human rights in development. At an *intrinsic* level, the growth in the formal acceptance of human rights law and the rate and number of ratification of legally binding agreements reveals the importance of human rights as foundational norms and values at the international level. The intrinsic value of human rights is that they establish a set of values, principles, and rights that are accepted unless they are explicitly negated.[40] The foundational and intrinsic importance of human rights is to explicate and interpret human dignity according to a set of norms, principles, and standards and to define formally and universally the thresholds below which human dignity is threatened or violated.

2. At the more *instrumental* level, a number of roles can be identified.

    ■ An important contribution of human rights to development concerns *empowerment*. Human rights frameworks and discourse facilitate self-reliance and the capacity to make claims by individuals and groups that might otherwise remain marginalized and powerless. The strengthening of freedom through the fulfillment of rights presumes channels for claims and advocacy, enabling demand-side accountability. Corruption and elite capture and control of resources may be less likely to happen in societies where respect for human rights exists.[41]

    ■ Also at an instrumental level, and a corollary to the empowerment dimension, is the *protection* that human rights afford individuals and groups in terms of integrity, freedom, equal treatment, and social safety nets. In developing countries such protection is also related to guaranteeing basic standards of

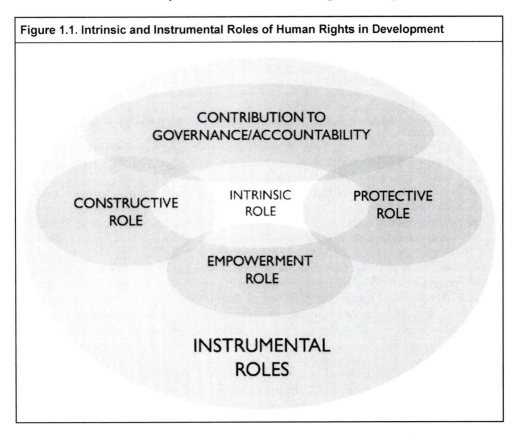

Figure 1.1. Intrinsic and Instrumental Roles of Human Rights in Development

CONTRIBUTION TO
GOVERNANCE/ACCOUNTABILITY

CONSTRUCTIVE
ROLE

INTRINSIC
ROLE

PROTECTIVE
ROLE

EMPOWERMENT
ROLE

INSTRUMENTAL
ROLES

welfare and to the establishment of structures of dispute resolution, legal aid mechanisms, and contract enforcement beyond the capital cities.

- The contribution of human rights to *accountability and governance* is increasingly recognized by donors and international agencies.[42] This strengthens arguments for instituting human rights dialogues with governments and civil society and for maintaining stronger human rights profiles in sector programs in health (e.g., HIV/AIDS), water, and education.[43]
- Human rights may play a *constructive* role as emphasized in Sen's conceptualization of development as freedom.[44] Freedoms of speech, association, movement, and the right to participate in public affairs sustain public debates on preferences and priorities and are essential for sustainable development.

Rights-Based Approaches to Development

Rights-based approaches to development feature prominently in discussions of the convergence of human rights and development.[45] The OHCHR has defined an RBA accordingly:

> A human rights-based approach is a conceptual framework for the process of human development that is normatively based on international human rights standards and operationally directed to promoting and protecting human rights. It seeks to analyse inequalities which lie at the heart of development problems and redress discriminatory practices and unjust distributions of power that impede development progress. Mere charity is not enough from a human rights perspective. Under a human rights-based approach, the plans, policies and processes of development are anchored in a system of rights and corresponding obligations established under international law. This helps to promote sustainability of development work, empowering people themselves—especially the most marginalized—to participate in policy formulation and accountable those who have a duty to act.[46]

The concept of a human rights–based approach is therefore broadly identified according to five basic principles:

- An anchoring of development efforts in human rights norms and standards and obligations
- A perspective that emphasizes analytical as well as operational approaches
- A perspective that focuses on participation and empowerment of rights-holders and on accountability of duty-bearers
- A focus on marginalized groups and on legal instruments that are especially relevant to them
- Assumptions about the centrality of inequality and discrimination as constraints on development progress

Rights-based development thus endeavors, on the one hand, to enhance human rights *respect, protection,* and *fulfilment* in developing countries as well as to *promote* human rights in development contexts and discourse. Rights-based approaches also argue that reliance on human rights rationales enhances development outcomes and development effectiveness, because human rights strategies target the root causes of poverty and have transformative goals. Thus, strategies for rights-based development are predicated on the assumption that the promotion and protection of human rights result in the general strengthening of development from both normative and operational perspectives, because human rights have an intrinsic and instrumental value in relation to achieving development goals. At the methodological level, RBA strategies emphasize (1) processes of enhancing empowerment of marginalized groups, (2) processes of enhancing accountability of duty-bearers, and (3) collaborative action between rights-holders and duty-bearers.[47] At a strategic and substantial level, rights-based approaches as they are implemented may underscore nondiscrimination, the realization of social rights as much as civil and political rights, and human rights work at local and district levels as components of development cooperation.

The contributions of a rights-based approach to development include providing a solid normative basis for values and policy choices that might otherwise be rendered more negotiable, a normative and legal baseline against which to check the quality of development processes and outcomes, the mandating of an essential minimum standard of enjoyment of rights, and a principle of "do no harm." RBAs offer legal and quasi-legal forms of recourse for violations or nonrealization of human rights in the context of development and a basis for accountability to states parties, but also to a wider range of actors in international development cooperation. RBAs result in the empowerment of poor people in contexts where their voice is not always heard and their autonomy not always respected; in this respect, RBAs help shift the focus of analysis to the most deprived and excluded. RBAs demand a deeper analysis of political and social *power relationships* in the public and private spheres, with the result that development programs that use RBAs are based on *ex ante* analyses of potential harm rather than being reactive in their approach to poverty and violent conflict.

RBAs are, however, not without their own set of difficulties or controversies. As a preliminary matter, there is no one rights-based approach, and the term RBA admits of multiple and competing definitions that may vary substantially across agencies.[48] RBAs are not easily embraced from the development side because of the large normative shift that they require, which often entails a view of poverty as a denial of human rights,[49] casting the net of potential responsibility (and blame) very wide indeed. RBAs presuppose the existence of human rights obligations and bring with them an inevitable political content, both of which are perceived as challenges in certain development circles. At a practical level too, RBAs demand a wholesale change of outlooks and operational frameworks development, requiring substantial training and resources. Such changes are more difficult to argue for when the empirical base and demonstrated value-added benefits of RBAs to traditional development objectives remain to be proven. Moreover, the implementation of RBAs has met significant hurdles, even in agencies with clear policy mandates and analytic bases to pursue them.

Tensions

Despite the complementary nature of human rights promotion and development strategies, important tensions persist between them, as summarized in table 1.1. The criticisms of development from the human rights side target an "accountability deficit" and the lack of normative standards against which to assess development processes and outcomes, as well as the primary and overriding economic focus of development policies. The issue of conditionality is a perennial feature of human rights critiques of international financial institutions and donors.[50] Governance programs also have been criticized as too closely tied to "supply-side politics" and public sector management and therefore as being inconsistent with human rights fulfilment.[51]

The scepticism expressed by development actors is not always explicit, but it is nevertheless influential: some challenge human rights accountability as both unrealistic and politically sensitive;[52] others view strengthened global or regional human rights regimes as an infringement of sovereignty[53] and at odds with state interests and policies;[54] still others, including some international and local NGOs, perceive international human rights as imposed on developing countries "from outside," designed to advance a Western or Northern neo-liberalist agenda.[55] As a result, the international human rights regime,

Table 1.1. Example of Potential Tension between Human Rights and Development Actors

Criticism raised by human rights advocates and scholars in relation to mainstream or traditional development approaches	Criticism raised by development scholars and actors in relation to human rights in development
▓ Insufficient accountability for development processes and outcomes ▓ Conditionality (impinging on the fulfilment of social rights and undermining domestic accountability) ▓ Supply-side governance focus ▓ Insufficient attention to legal accountability ▓ "Do no harm" neglected ▓ Inadequate participation, consultation, and ownership of development processes ▓ Excessive focus on purely economic dimensions of poverty, not enough on social and equity dimensions	▓ Conditionality (political, effectiveness) ▓ Enlarging agendas of human rights accountability ▓ North to South imposition of human rights norms and values ▓ Sovereignty infringement ▓ Risks of bypassing government counterparts ▓ Open politicization of development processes and institutions ▓ Human rights "capacity deficit" within development agencies—lack of comparative advantage

Source: The authors.

though strengthened considerably during the 1990s in terms of scope and institutional proliferation, remains inconsistent in its application to development,[56] and its impacts in that field are not well documented.

Notes

[1] Jack Donnelly, 2003. *Universal Human Rights in Theory and Practice*, 2d ed. (Ithaca, Cornell University Press) 7. See also Jack Donnelly, 1993. *International Human Rights* (Boulder, Westview Press) 19.

[2] Maurice Cranston, 1973. *What Are Human Rights?* (Taplinger Publishing Co.) 36. See also Jack Donnelly, 1985. *The Concept of Human Rights* (London, Croom Helm). And Louis Henkin, 1981. Introduction in *The International Bill of Rights* (Passim, Columbia University Press).

[3] Theodore Meron, 1986. "On a Hierarchy of International Human Rights: Discussing the Hierarchical Terminology in International Human Rights," In *Am. Journal of International Law*, 80.

[4] Robert Ian Brownlie, 2008. *Principles of Public International Law* (Oxford, OUP) 553–584 , and on customary or general international law, see 562–564.

[5] At least some of the provisions of the Universal Declaration of Human Rights are accepted as binding customary international law. See Hurst Hannum, 1995–1996. *Ga. J. Int'l & Comp. Law. The Status of the Universal Declaration of Human Rights* in *National and International Law* 25. 287; Louis Henkin, 1990. *The Age of Rights* (New York, Colombia University Press) 19.

[6] See Appendix A. The OHCHR classifies these as core international human rights instruments. The International Convention for the Protection of All Persons from Enforced Disappearances is not yet in force.

[7] The international instruments that explicitly link human rights and development are, however, not legally binding, e.g., the 1986 Declaration on the Right to Development; Report of the Human Rights Council 2nd Session to 4th Session (New York, 2007). General Assembly, Official Records 62th session, Supplement No. 53 (A/62/53).

[8] See Amartya Sen, 1999. *Development as Freedom* (Oxford, OUP) World Bank Comprehensive Development Framework. http://web.worldbank.org/WBSITE/EXTERNAL/PROJECTS/STRATEGIES/CDF/0,,pagePK:60447~theSitePK:140576,00.html.

[9] See e.g., World Bank Group http://ddp-ext.worldbank.org/ext/GMIS/gdmis.do?siteId=2&menuId=LNAV01HOME1
See also The World Bank and IMF Joint Development Committee, 2006. *Global Monitoring Report 2006. Aid Trade and Governance.* (Washington DC 2006-0004).

[10] Launched under World Bank president Wolfensohn in 1999. See e.g., www.worldbank.org/cdf.

[11] See World Bank, 2004. Social Development Strategy. www.worldbank.org.

[12] UNDP defined human development as a process of enlarging people's choices, *Human Development Report*, 1990. See also *supra n.* 8.

[13] See André Frankovits and Patrick Earle, 2001. *The Rights Way to Development. A Human Rights Approach to Development Assistance. Policy and Practice.* (Marrickvill, The Human Rights Council of Australia) 25.

[14] See Secretary General's Report, 1997. *Renewing the United Nations: A Programme for Reform,* UN Doc. A/51/950 and see UN Secretary-General, General Assembly, 2005. *In Larger Freedom. towards Development, Security and Human Rights for All.* A/59/2005.

[15] Varun Gauri, 2004. *Social and Economic Rights: Claims to Health Care and Education in Developing Countries.* World Development, Vol. 32, Issue 3, 465–477. Varun Gauri and Daniel M. Brinks (Eds.), 2008. *Social and Economic Rights in Developing Countries. Politics, Law and Impact* (Cambridge, Cambridge University Press).

[16] See e.g., OECD DAC, 2007. *Action-Oriented Policy Paper on Human Rights and Development.* (OECD). For an interpretation of the human rights and development convergence during the late 1990s, see Hans-Otto Sano, 2000. *Development and Human Rights. The Necessary, but Partial Integration of Human Rights and Development.* Human Rights Quarterly. Vol. 22, No. 3. 734–752.

[17] OHCHR, Report of the OHCHR on the Relationship between Climate Change and Human Rights, U.N. Doc. A/HRC/10/61 (ja. 15, 2009); U.N. Human Rights Council Res. 10/4 in UNHRC Draft Report of the Human Rights Council on its 10th Session 13 U.N. Doc A/HRC/10/L.11 (March 31, 2009).

[18] Although the Millennium Declaration contained such references, the Goals as the operative part of the MDG framework did not. See also Philip Alston, 2005. "Ships Passing in the Night: The Current State of the Human Rights and Development Debate Seen through the Lens of the Millennium Development Goals" Human Rights Quarterly. Vol. 27, 755–829. The gap is also manifest in the existence of a second and a third standing committee of the UN General Assembly, dealing with sustainable development and human rights, respectively, or disconnects between the representation of governments in development institutions and human rights institutions.

[19] *Ibid.* 826

[20] See *supra n.* 17. Mary Robinson & Philip Alston, 2005 (Eds.) *Human Rights and Development: Towards Mutual Reinforcement.* Especially introduction; M. Nowak, 2002. "A Human Rights Approach to Poverty" in Human Rights in Development Yearbook. *Empowerment, Participation, Accountability and Non-Discrimination,* Martin Scheinin and Markku Suks (Eds.) 2005. *Operationalising Human Rights-Based Approaches to Development* (Leiden/Boston, Martinus Nijhoff Publishers) (Nordic Human Rights Publications, Oslo) 17–35; Mac Darrow and Amparo Thomas, 2005. "Power, Capture, and Conflict: A Call for Human Rights Accountability in Development Cooperation" in *Human Rights Law Quarterly.* Vol. 27; Klaus Decker, Siobhán McInerney-Lankford, Caroline Sage, *Human Rights and Equitable Development: "Ideals," Issues and Implications.* Background paper to the WDR 2006 available at: http://go.worldbank.org/3AN4HQ0SC0.

[21] OECD-DAC Govnet, 2006. *Integrating Human Rights into Development, Donor Approaches, Experiences and Challenges.* (Paris, OECD), 25–36.

[22] Mary Robinson and Philip Alston, 2004. *Human Rights and Development: Towards Mutual Reinforcement* (Oxford, OUP).

[23] UNDG, 2003. *The Human Rights-Based Approach to Development Cooperation. Towards a Common Understanding among the UN Agencies.* 2003. (Stamford, CT), also referred to as the *Stamford Declaration.*

[24] The World Bank is a member and co-chair of this Task Team.

[25] Those principles are the following:
1. Build a shared understanding of the links between human rights obligations and development priorities through dialogue.
2. Identify areas of support to partner governments on human rights.
3. Safeguard human rights in processes of state-building.
4. Support the demand side of human rights.
5. Promote nondiscrimination as a basis for more inclusive and stable societies.
6. Consider human rights in decisions on alignment and aid instruments.
7. Consider mutual reinforcement between human rights and aid effectiveness principles.
8. Do no harm.
9. Take a harmonized and graduated approach to deteriorating human rights situations.
10. Ensure that the scaling-up of aid is conducive to human rights.

[26] OECD DAC Human Rights and Aid Effectiveness documents. http://www.oecd.org/document/4/0,3343,en_2649_3236398_45493060_1_1_1_1,00.html The work now includes Draft Principles on Aid Effectiveness and Human Rights (2009).

[27] Regulation (EC) No. 1889/2006 of the European Parliament and of the Council of December 20, 2006. "On Establishing a Financing Instrument for the Promotion of Democracy and Human Rights Worldwide." *Official Journal of the European Union* 29.12.2006 L 386. See also European Commission, External Relations, 2007. *Furthering Human Rights and Democracy across the Globe.* (Bruxelles and Luxembourg).

[28] A similar approach was articulated by the then General Counsel, Ibrahim Shihata, 2000. "The World Bank and Human Rights – A Presentation before the 1993 UN World Conference on Human Rights" in *The World Bank Legal Papers*, 815, in which he states: "My purpose today is to highlight the contribution of the World Bank to the promotion of human rights, to emphasize the complementarity of the respect for human rights and human development in general."

[29] *Ibid.*

[30] "The Bank's operations attempt in fact to help its borrowers to transform the economic and social rights proclaimed in the Universal Declaration of Human rights an the in the International Covenant on Economic, Social and Cultural rights from ideals into realities […]Ibrahim Shihata, *'The World Bank and Human Rights – A Presentation. Before the 1993 World Conference on Human Rights,'* in The World Bank Legal Papers (2000):815, 816 and at 817.

[31] World Bank, 1998, *Development and Human Rights: the Role of the World* Bank http://www .worldbank.org/html/extdr/rights/hrtext.pdf

[32] *Ibid.*

[33] *Ibid.*

[34] More information available at http://go.worldbank.org/PKPTI6FU40 visited on 3/29/2010.

[35] Roberto Dañino, 2005, "Legal Aspects of the World Bank's Work on Human Rights: Some Preliminary Thoughts" in Mary Robinson and Philip Alston (Eds.), *Human Rights and Development: Towards Mutual Reinforcement.* See also *supra n.* 22 at 510, 571. and 524.

[36] Roberto Dañino, 2006. *The Legal Aspects of the World Bank's Work on Human Rights* in Development Outreach, October 2006.

[37] Ana Palacio, 2006. "The Way Forward: Human Rights and the World Bank" in *Development Outreach*, October 2006.

[38] On "rhetorical incorporation," see Peter Uvin, 2004. *Human Rights and Development* (Bloomfield, Kumarian Press) 50.

[39] International Bank for Reconstruction and Development Articles of Agreement (amended February 16, 1989) available at http://siteresources.worldbank.org/EXTABOUTUS/Resources/ibrd -articlesofagreement.pdf .

[40] See Amartya Sen, 1999. "Democracy as a Universal Value" in *Journal of Democracy*, Vol. 10. No. 3.

[41] See Daniel Kaufman, 2005. "Human Rights and Governance: The Empirical Challenge" in Philip Alston and Mary Robinson, *Human Rights and Development: Towards Mutual Reinforcement* (Oxford, OUP).

[42] See *supra n. 16*

[43] See Hans-Otto Sano, 2007. "Does a Human Rights-Based Approach Make a Difference?" In Margot Salomon, Arne Tostensen, and Wouter Vandenhole, 2007. *Casting the Net Wider: Human Rights, Development and New Duty-Bearers.* (Antwerp, Intersentia).

[44] See *supra* n. 8.

[45] In this paper, occasional use is made of the acronym RBA for rights-based approaches.

[46] OHCHR (Office of the High Commissioner for Human Rights), 2006. *Frequently Asked Questions on a Human Rights-Based Approach to Development Cooperation* (Geneva; New York, United Nations).

[47] For a description of these methodological contributions, see Sano *supra n.* 43. See also Paul Gready, 2009. "Reasons to Be Cautious about Evidence and Evaluation: Rights-Based Approaches to Development and the Emerging Culture of Evaluation," *Journal of Human Rights Practice*, 1 (3), 380–401.

[48] Celestine Nyamu-Musembi and Andrea Cornwall, 2004. *What Is the "Rights-Based Approach" All About? Perspectives from International Development Agencies.* IDS Working Paper No 234 (Brighton, IDS) 13–15.

[49] Some advocate an even stronger characterization of violation, rather than denial.

[50] A study focusing particularly on elections was Katarina Tomsevski, 1999. *Between Sanctions and Elections. Aid Donors and Their Human Rights Performance* (London, Pinter). A more recent study examining conditionality in the EU context is Lorand Bartels, 2005. *Human Rights Conditionality in the*

EU's International Agreements (Oxford, OUP) 37. One conclusion from this study was that EU mainly imposed sanctions against the poorest countries in the South, usually in connection with military coups.

[51] Mette Kjær and Klavs Kinnerup, 2002. "Good Governance: How does it Relate to Human Rights?" In Hans-Otto Sano and Gudmundur Alfredsson (Eds.) *Human Rights and Good Governance. Building Bridges.* (Den Hauge, Martinus Nijhoff, Brill).

[52] *See* Andrew Clapham, 2006. *Human Rights Obligations of Non-State Actors* (Oxford, OUP). Margot E. Solomon, 2007. "International Economic Governance and Human Rights Accountability" In M. Salomon, A. Tostenson, and V. Vandenhole (Eds.) *Casting the Net Wider: Human Rights, Development and New Duty-Bearers* (Antwerp, Intersentia).

[53] In the eyes of development actors, and especially perhaps among the donors, human rights promotion and protection touches on political dimensions, especially in relation to sovereignty, where these actors prefer to tread lightly. The agenda of legal accountability inherent in human rights obligations may pose challenges, for instance sovereignty and transnational obligations. Among donors themselves, development assistance is not considered as a human rights obligation that they have to fulfil in accordance with legal obligations incurred under the conventions. The obligations under customary international law are mainly negative, i.e., linked to principles of doing no human rights harm. Yet the authors of the covenant on economic, social, and cultural rights and the convention on the rights of the child envisaged that the fulfilment of these rights could be linked to international cooperation. See Sigrun Skogly and Mark Gibney, 2002. "Transnational Human Rights Obligations," in *Human Rights Quarterly.* Vol. 24. 781–798.

[54] David P. Forsythe, 2000. *Human Rights in International Relations. Supra* note 34. 55–56, 135–136, and 159–160. Stéphanie Lagoutte, Hans-Otto Sano, and Peter Scharff Smith, 2007. *Human Rights in Turmoil. Facing Threats, Consolidating Achievements* (Martinus Nijhoff).

[55] Daniel A. Bell and Jean-Marc Coicaud, 2006. *Ethics in Action. The Ethical Challenges of Human Rights-Nongovernmental Organizations* (Cambridge, Cambridge University Press, and United Nations University).

[56] David P. Forsythe, 2000. *Human Rights in International Relations* (Cambridge, Cambridge University Press) 55–56, 135–136, and 159–160.

CHAPTER 3

Human Rights Indicators

Introduction

Indicators serve different purposes. They are used as a means to summarize a situation, i.e., to gain an insight into broader trends of development or of other social phenomena. In this respect, indicators are analytical. However, indicators are also used to assess compliance by parties with specific targets or obligations. In this way, indicators are used to measure accountability to norms, standards, or stated policies. Finally, indicators are used to assess performance in relation to planned objectives, such as the effectiveness of programs and projects. In the human rights field, a principal focus is to assess compliance with human rights obligations and to examine human rights accountability.

Why are human rights indicators important? First, they link the conceptual discussion about human rights compliance to implementation practices. They link the normative level of international legal obligation with the practical level of empirical data. At a different level, the employment of human rights indicators in development practice implies some form of human rights mainstreaming or some effort to integrate human rights.

Box 1.1 contains definitions of indicators that range from those emphasizing achievements and performance (OECD) to more general definitions based on indicators as signposts of a situation or development (Radstaake and Bronkhorst). The working definition of this paper is the last definition, relied upon because it embodies a concern with indicators as signposts, i.e., as pieces of information that may provide insight into matters of larger significance. It also possesses two characteristics that apply to *all* indicators:

1. First, they are *data that have been created or transformed and used by organizations and institutions*, or by analysts, for different purposes. In this sense, they are also *communicative instruments*, e.g. used for accountability, certification, or quality control. If indicators have no institutional legitimacy or ownership, i.e., if institutions or researchers do not endorse and use them, they are not indicators, but just data.
2. A second characteristic of indicators is that they are *tools of measurement* the purpose of which may range from the simple assessment of achievement to more complex and conceptually demanding examination of compliance and signposting of social change. As *planning tools,* they provide a means for scrutinizing performance. As means of *compliance measurement,* they demand conceptual rigor and authoritative interpretation. As signposting means of "summing up" and "measuring change instruments," they depend on theoretical insight that allows broader conceptualization, such as accepted methodologies of measuring human development or good governance.

Designing Indicators

The political choices and theoretical premises underpinning the design of indicators typically remain implicit. The way in which they are formulated, as either quantitative or

---

Box 3.1. Indicator Definitions

"Indicator: Quantitative or qualitative factor or variable that provides a simple and reliable means to measure achievement, to reflect the changes connected to an intervention, or to help assess the performance of a development actor."[1] (OECD Development Assistance Committee)

"Indicators are pieces of information that provide insight into matters of larger significance and make perceptible trends that are not immediately detectable."[2] (Abbot and Gujit)

"Technically speaking, an indicator refers to a set of statistics that can serve as a proxy or a metaphor for phenomena that are not directly measurable. However, the term is often used less precisely to mean any data pertaining to social conditions."[3] (Green)

Indicators: "The aggregated and combined summaries of facts, as 'signposts' for what a situation is and how it is developing. For example the existence of freely operating political parties and of major newspapers that are not controlled by the state is an indicator of the observance of civil liberties. Indicators may be strictly quantitative (such as the UNDP Human Development Index), largely qualitative, or a mix of both."[4] (Radstaake and Bronkhorst)

"Indicators are data used by analysts or institutions and organizations to describe situations that exist or to measure changes or trends over a period of time. They are communicative descriptions of conditions or of performance that may provide insights into matters of larger significance beyond what is actually measured."[5] (Andersen and Sano)

---

qualitative statements, depends largely on the character, type, and purpose of indicators, as well as the sources of data available. Designing indicators in a quantitative format allows either comparison or the assessment according to a standardized norm or benchmark, such as *"Ensure that all boys and girls complete a full course of primary schooling."*

The practice of human rights actors in development reveals little consistency in the formulation of indicators. A bewildering diversity prevails, whether actors are focusing on duty-bearer compliance at the macro-level or on performance of planned development change at the micro-level. One overriding challenge is therefore how to establish greater consistency in the design of indicators to facilitate horizontal comparisons between countries or between state parties. Alternatively, more consistent employment of indicators may also be achieved in efforts of vertical integration, in which indicators of planned change at the micro-level are used and compared to a country specific benchmark or targets.

Streamlining Human Rights Indicators

There is widespread caution about the use of human rights indicators facilitating country comparison or ranking in development. This was evident at the conference on Statics, Development and Human Rights in Montreux during 2000, and it continued to be reiterated within the OECD-sponsored Metagora Project[6] measuring governance, democracy, and human rights. The resistance relates to obvious political sensitivities, but also to methodological concerns about underestimating the diversity between countries (the so-called variance truncation), although embedded in human rights approaches to mediate this issue is the principle of cultural relativism, which stresses the specificity and diversity of contexts.[7] Greater receptivity is evident in relation to the vertical streamlining of indicators. In 2002, OHCHR circulated *The Draft Guidelines on a Human Rights Approach to Poverty Reduction Strategies.*[8] This document contains not only human rights–based indicators, but also targets linked to the indicators. The integration of targets or benchmarks facilitates vertical integration between macro- and micro-level indicators, e.g., between country-level compliance assessment and program- or project-level performance indicators; the existence of targets could provide a framework for common indicator sets.

Donors increasingly combine the formulation of indicators with the definition of specific targets. Examples include the framework underpinning the Paris Declaration on Aid Effectiveness[9] or in the linking of targets to the MDG indicators.[10] In the latter context, there are several examples that states, donors, and NGOs streamline their activities according to the goals, indicators, and targets. In the former, indicators and targets become tools of mainstreaming policies and activities. Greater consistency may therefore be gained by translating indicators into targets. Moreover, consistent targets and indicators may also provide better incentives for assessment. However, targeting may have potential drawbacks as well, especially in promoting a lean approach to indicator formulation, in which the resultant indicators have little substance. Such performance measures demonstrate that accomplishments were made according to plan, but the underlying rationale for choosing one target over another, or the relationship of particular targets to an understanding of substantive impact, may not always be clear. Furthermore, targeting relates more to specific results than to process, the latter being central to human rights assessment. Thus, unless the assessment is related to more substantive discussions of process and results, an assessment of target achievements may have limited use.

Data Sources[11]

The data sources of human rights research may be quantitative or qualitative. They may range from interviews with vulnerable groups to expert assessment of the situation with respect to a particular standard. The data underpinning human rights indicators are often expert-based or are based on domestic law or administrative regulation, whereas few regular and comprehensive survey sources are used in human rights assessment. Official statistics are rarely used in definition of national indicators because such sources have few rights-relevant data, although, at the national level, official statistics may increasingly cooperate with human rights institutions in order to establish the relevant data bases.[12] At the international level, the statistical deficits are partly due to the fact that a framework of conceptualizing human rights has been missing—a fact that may be remedied by the consensus achieved on the OHCHR indicators discussed in the following. In the field of economic, social, and cultural rights, the emerging consensus that certain MDG indicators are also human rights indicators implies that international comparative data are available in which MDG indicators overlap with economic and social rights. Thus, although not all data are indicators, the emerging understanding and consensus on human rights indicators may also create a demand for new types of data.

There are ongoing debates about the overlaps between human rights and development indicators and about what distinguishes a human rights indicator from other indicators.[13] This debate stems, at least in part, from concerns about using available development data in a human rights context and is closely linked to efforts aimed at measuring compliance with economic, social, and cultural rights and using socioeconomic data in the latter context.[14] A central question in this connection is therefore this: When do particular data become a piece of human rights statistic?

Two quotes serve to illustrate the challenge and dilemma. In the OHCHR *Draft Guidelines on a Human Rights Approach to Poverty Reduction,* from 2003, it was argued that

> most of the indicators proposed in these Guidelines are standard indicators of socioeconomic progress, although it should be observed that some human rights indicators, especially those relating to civil and political rights, do not usually figure in measures of socio-economic progress. Essentially, what distinguishes a human rights indicator from a standard disaggregated indicator of socio-economic progress is less its substance than (a) its explicit derivation from a human rights norm and (b) the purpose to which it is put, namely human rights monitoring with a view to holding duty-bearers to account.[15]

Box 3.2. The Data Sources of Human Rights Research[16]

Survey data sources: data collected as part of sample surveys or using structured questionnaire approaches.

Official statistical sources based on sample surveys, censuses,

Perception surveys sources: data collected with the specific purpose of soliciting interpretations and qualitative statements by stakeholders or target groups. Perception surveys are being undertaken in a number of developing countries as part of so-called barometer surveys in which perceptions of poverty or of democracy and transparency are being measured.

Expert assessment: interpretation of human rights situation based on expert sources.

Qualitative interviews: data collected as part of focus group or other types of interview processes.

Administrative data sources: data collected from public administrations and organizations.

Event-based studies: data documenting human rights violations (what happened, who did what to whom?).[17]

Conversely, Landman and Häusermann 2003 argue:

> in the absence of clear economic and social rights indicators, attention is being paid to using or adapting development indicators. The strength in using development indicators for human rights measurement lies in their regular availability, global coverage, ease of understanding and long time-series . . . The key weakness in using development indicators for human rights measurement is the serious question of their validity. For example, using literacy rates, educational attainment, gender breakdown in education, and investment in schools only demonstrates the state of education in a particular country <u>not</u> whether the right to freedom from discrimination in education is being upheld.[18]

Thus, although one source argues that there are two criteria of valid human rights indicators—derivation from a rights-based norm and the purpose of using the data to assess duty-holders' human rights accountability—the other argues that valid human rights indicators must measure core human rights principles, such as freedom from discrimination. Under the latter view, "the ratio of boys to girls in primary schools" is not a human rights indicator. The approaches embody broad and restrictive definitions of what qualify as valid human rights indicators.

More recently, agreement has converged around the former position, favoring a broader definition of human rights indicators. Thus, the OHCHR work includes outcome indicators that overlap with MDG indicators, e.g., an indicator such as "proportion of underweight children below five." The peculiarity of human rights indicators according to this interpretation is not that discrimination is embodied in every indicator, nor that human rights language enters into the specific formulation of the indicator, but rather that the indicators are employed for purposes of assessing human rights accountability or for purposes of assessing the presence of human rights principles.

Another peculiar trait of human rights indicators is that, in contrast to development indicators, they devote particular attention to *process* and *conduct*. Development indicators have tended to focus on *outcomes*, whereas human rights indicators, because of the emphasis on accountability, underscore the relevance of processes. *"Human development monitoring focuses on human outcomes (result) while human rights gives particular emphasis on the fulfilment of obligations (conduct) Human rights emphasize concerns with effectiveness of state policies, and the obligation of other actors, with eliminating discrimination and achieving equitable development, with participation and progress rather than absolute level. Human rights bring new concepts such as effective remedy and accountability which enrich development debates considerably."*[19]

Types of Human Rights Indicators

This chapter surveys different types of indicators without purporting to provide an exhaustive analysis. A primary focus is placed on compliance indicators and compliance assessment, although there is some consideration of planned performance indicators and how they are used at the micro-level. In contrasting the latter with compliance indicators, some insights may be gained concerning the nature and practice of human rights measurement.

Indicators Measuring Compliance with Legal Obligations

After prolonged debates on human rights indicators and their typology, an emerging consensus is discernable at the international level. Beginning in 2005, under the aegis of the OHCHR, a group of experts has developed a typology of *structure, process,* and *outcome* indicators inspired in part by the previous work of the Special Rapporteur, on the right to the highest attainable standard of physical and mental health. The purpose of the exercise has been to provide the U.N. human rights treaty bodies[20] with a methodology and conceptual framework for monitoring compliance by state parties with international human rights treaties.[21] The exercise is designed also to assist states in their reporting duties under the treaties and to improve the quality and consistency of reports submitted.

By early 2010, the following tasks had been accomplished. First, illustrative indicators have been identified on a number of human rights and thematic issues and subjected to validation. These indicators facilitate the identification and use of contextually relevant indicators through appropriate country-level participatory processes. At present, illustrative indicators are available for the following rights:

- Right to life
- Right to liberty and security of person
- Right to participate in public affairs
- Right not to be subjected to torture or cruel, inhuman, or degrading treatment or punishment
- Right to the enjoyment of the highest attainable standard of physical and mental health
- Right to adequate food
- Right to adequate housing
- Right to education
- Right to freedom of opinion and expression
- Right to a fair trial
- Right to social security
- Right to work
- Right to nondiscrimination and equality
- Violence against women

Meta-data sheets, namely detailed information on identified indicators (definition, rationale, method of computation, sources, disaggregation levels, periodicity, plus any other relevant information facilitating interpretation and use of indicators) have also been developed for selected indicators and included as an appendix to the report HRI/MC/2008/3.

A guide will be developed during 2010–11 that is intended to help reporting governments, as duty-bearers, under the relevant treaties, in the use of the indicators developed. This tool is intended to address interpretative challenges that may be encountered in the application of indicators.

The methodology consists first of defining four or five attributes of the rights in question, i.e., the characteristic domains of each right identified by the treaty bodies or in other authoritative interpretations.[22] Indicators for each right are then examined at three levels—structural, process, and outcome—and defined according to attributes and levels.

Structural indicators are defined as the ratification or adoption of legal instruments, national policy instruments and statement and existence of basic institutional mechanisms deemed necessary for facilitating realization of the concerned human right. They reflect the legal and institutional framework for the implementation of human rights, including the national policy statements on a given right. These indicators address the macro-level formal acceptance of a right, including legislation and regulations adopted to implement treaty obligations under international human rights law.

Process indicators relate state policy instruments with outcome indicators. State policy instruments refer to a range of measures including public programs and specific interventions that a state is willing to take in order to give effect to its intent or commitments to attain outcomes identified with the realization of a given human right. By defining the process indicators in terms of a concrete cause and effect relationship, the accountability of the state to its obligations can be better assessed. These indicators also help monitor the progressive fulfilment or protection of a right. Process indicators are more sensitive to changes than outcome indicators and are therefore more effective in capturing the progressive realization of the right or in reflecting the efforts of the state parties in protecting the rights

Outcome indicators capture attainments or results, whether individual and collective, that reflect the status of realization of human rights in a given context. It is not only a more direct measure of the realization of a human right but it also reflects the importance of measurement of the enjoyment of the right. In this, it reflects the culmination of a process of formal acceptance of a legal obligation, through the processes required for the realization of rights, to the end enjoyment of the right. Because the outcome consolidates the impact of various underlying processes over time (which can be captured by one or more process indicators), an outcome indicator is often a slow-moving indicator, less sensitive to capturing momentary changes than a process indicator. For example, life expectancy or mortality indicator could be a function of immunization of population, education, or public health awareness of the population, as well as availability and accessibility of individuals to adequate nutrition.[23]

These distinctions are useful in providing a structure for compliance assessment. The OHCHR indicators seek to capture *legal and policy acceptance* of human rights, the *effort* of duty-bearers in terms of rights realization, and *attainments in terms of actual human rights enjoyment.*[24] The division of structure, process, and outcome reveals how human rights indicators can be categorized into different types of indicators. These divisions can be seen in the light of obligations of different types inherent in human rights, i.e., the obligations to respect, protect, and fulfil rights of duty-bearers, although this tripartite distinction is not used in the OHCHR description of the indicators. Table 3.1 illustrates these elements by building upon the OHCHR framework. The vertical axis lists types of indicators described in the previous chapter: *structure, process and outcome* indicators. Process or outcome indicators can, moreover, be described in terms of *effort or result*, respectively.[25] On the horizontal axis, the table depicts duty-bearer accountabilities in terms of the tripartite division, which is used in human rights thinking to describe the nature of human rights obligations, namely respect, protect, and fulfil.[26] The horizontal axis also includes, however, columns on the legal framework and on the existing channels of redress. This dimension is closely connected to structural indicators and to the capacity to fulfil human rights obligations. The table therefore seeks to capture how types of human rights indicators relate to duty-bearer obligations and to fundamental dimensions of legal acceptance.

In assessing the OHCHR work, a number of points emerge:

■ Overall, the work is aimed at facilitating compliance assessment—in particular, that conducted by the U.N. human rights treaty bodies. Although indicators must

Table 3.1. A Framework for the Elaboration of Human Rights Indicators

| | Legal Framework | Nature of Duty-Bearer Accountability | | |
		Respect	Protect	Fulfil
Structure *Acceptance*	Indicators of ratification, national law, general policy acceptance and statements	Content of laws upholding human rights (especially negative clauses)	Content of laws regarding third-party actions that may impinge human rights	Content of laws or policies that positively advance human rights
Process *Effort* Process indicators reflect duty-bearers' efforts of improving system performance effectiveness of access, redress, nondiscrimination, equity, and participation	Indicators measuring efforts of enhancing, e.g., the effectiveness of the judicial system	Indicators capturing duty-bearer efforts to refrain from interfering with rights, i.e., measuring preventive efforts in relation to state institutions and actors committing human rights violations	Indicators capturing duty-bearer efforts to address third-party human rights violations and interference with rights	Indicators capturing duty-bearer human rights facilitation, promotion, and positive resource allocation for rights realization
Outcome *Result* Outcome indicators reflect actual enjoyment of human rights standards and principles by individuals and groups	Indicators measuring the effectiveness and efficiency of the judiciary and of access to justice	Status of rights-holder enjoyment of rights	Status of rights-holder protection from third-party violation	Status in terms of provision or promotion of human rights obligations for individuals and groups

Source: The authors.

still be contextualized into domestic country situations, the framework offers a conceptual model and provides a set of illustrative indicators relevant to particular human rights under U.N. human rights treaties.

■ The formulation and thrust of the indicators is aligned to more positive or facilitative and progressive realization than to negative assessments of violations.[27] Even outcome indicators relating to civil and political rights are rarely defined in a way that could focus directly on human rights violations.

■ The exercise reflects some consensus on the importance of measuring civil and political as well as economic, social, and cultural rights, but it has yet to be institutionalized in the practices of the U.N. human rights treaty bodies.

■ The expert group has found it consistent with human rights law to give a number of human rights indicators similar definitions to MDG indicators. As a result, for some human rights indicators, data are already available as a result of the MDG monitoring, which may in turn facilitate compliance assessment of social rights.

■ A significant output of the exercise is its definition of process indicators. The focus on duty-bearer commitment or effort may be one of the areas in which human rights indicators are distinct from development indicators. However, the definition of process measurement in the indicator tables elaborated by the expert group so far[28] illustrates some of the challenges involved. Process indicators are given multiple definitions: first, as "milestones on a path to outcome indicators"; second, in definitions associated with complaints mechanisms, and third, as measures of public policies and programmes that may reveal a state's intention to attain outcomes identified with the realization of a given human right.

Beyond indicators developed for binding human rights under treaties, it is worth mentioning those developed in the work of the U.N. High Level Task Force on the Right to Development (HLTF)[29] between 2004–2010. Part of the mandate of the HLTF is "(a) to monitor and review progress made in the promotion and implementation of the right to development as elaborated in the Declaration on the Right to Development, at the national and international levels, [. . .]"[30] In pursuance of that, the HLTF has developed criteria and subcriteria to address the essential features of the right to development, as defined in the Declaration on the Right to Development. Its methodology involved the elaboration of (1) a general statement on the basic expectation of the right to development (its "core norm"); (2) a clarification of the core norm through the enumeration of three attributes of the right; (3) the development of several criteria to assess the realization of attributes; (4) the development of subcriteria to facilitate the precision of criteria; (5) the subcriteria may then be assessed by drawing upon reliable measurement tools in the form of one or several indicators.[31] The basic methodology developed by the HLTF builds in part on the OHCHR exercise on human rights indicators, but with some additional layers of nuance and incorporation of development indicators presumably integrated because of the generality of the right to development in comparison with the treaty rights examined by the OHCHR (see Appendix G).

Human Rights Indicators in Development Practice

Human rights–related activities are undertaken at a number of different levels in development, whether by donor agencies, U.N. organizationsm or IFIs. A growing number of international and local NGOs are also involved in human rights–related development activities. Yet the human rights indicator practices of these organizations and institutional actors remain unarticulated and widely divergent.

Human rights indicators are therefore relevant not only in relation to state compliance with treaty obligations, as discussed previously, but also potentially in relation to program- or project-level development policies and practice. This chapter describes a range of approaches that can be identified to human rights indicators in development practice at various levels, which are illustrated in table 3.2. Distinctions are made between the following:

Compliance measurement, indicating respect for principles and rights. Compliance can be negative, refraining from infringements, or positive—fulfilling and sustaining a given rights regime.
Performance assessment, indicating implementation processes toward goals, milestones, or targets.

From top to bottom, table 3.2 illustrates how indicators are developed at global, regional, sector, and program levels. The distinction between compliance and performance is not always clear-cut, but performance measures are typical of process assessment, whether in relation to targets or in relation to realization of specific goals. At the global level, a more legalistic and treaty-based use of human rights indicators is evident. At the regional or sector levels, methodologies are institutionally and thematically defined, whereas at program and project levels, indicators are more contextualized and varied, defined according to the specific aims of the program or project. The gradation of purposes is illustrative of the challenges involved in the creation of consistent indicators. At the top level is the measurement of human rights accountability through compliance assessment, such as that proposed by the

OHCHR. It is based on legal accountability and the commitments of states under public international law. This methodology also represents a positive approach to human rights indicators—inasmuch as the focus on human rights violations is less pronounced and greater emphasis is placed on government effort and on outcome indicators of progressive realization.[32] This contrasts with a violations-based approach such as that of the CIRI Human Rights Data Project, which focuses on the degree to which state duty-bearers fail to live up to their human rights obligations and which may therefore be characterized as a more negative approach. In addition, the CIRI approach presents opportunities for comparative assessment, which some criticize as a ranking methodology.

Further down the chart, the Millennium Development Goals have given rise to the formulation of both indicators and joint targets. Similarly, the approach developed for monitoring of the Paris Declaration employs targets and indicators. The indicator for ownership, for example, is the following: *"Number of countries with national development strategies (including PRSs) that have clear strategic priorities linked to a medium-term expenditure framework and reflected in annual budgets."* The target of this indicator for 2010 is defined as "At least 75% of partner countries have operational development strategies." This methodology, linked to measurable and verifiable targets that are used for all development assistance, represents the characteristic way in which indicators are being converted into targets. Moreover, the effort to define common indicators to measure joint performance between state governments and donors represents new and interesting approaches to indicator definition. At the level where institutional methodologies are relevant, the indicators tend not to be based on human right standards, even when they relate to human rights substantively. The CPIA measurement by the World Bank is one such example. It includes criteria and indicators on social inclusion and equity, gender equality, social protection, and labor. Performance on the CPIA scale is linked to the allocation of resources for IDA eligible countries (although the instrument fulfils other functions within the Bank in terms of general country monitoring).

The *European Civic and Inclusion Index*, which during 2007 was retitled as *Migrant Integration Policy Index*, is an example of regionally based methodologies that are not standard-based. A first preliminary methodology was published 2003, followed by a more elaborate report including country assessments in 2005 and in 2007.[33] The index is not development-oriented, but the methodology is development relevant. It benchmarks laws and policies according to key issues in which scoring assessment is based on expert assessment. The issues assessed are labor market inclusion, long-term residence, family reunion, nationality, and antidiscrimination. Assessment according to these subjects provides the foundation for scoring and index values. Although the scoring methodology may be debated, the benchmarking methodology represents an interesting example of how methods of assessing discriminatory laws or policies can be refined.

The two last examples in table 3.2 illustrate use of indicators related to programming methodologies, i.e., to goal attainment under development programs. Human rights programs financed by NGOs or by donors are often based on logical framework concepts relying on indicators that measure short- and medium-term goal attainment. Under rights-based programming, indicators often relate to processes of empowerment, nondiscrimination, participation, and accountability by duty-bearers. The programming field offers diverse examples of human rights–based or human rights–related indicators (which points to a distinction of some relevance). PRS programs use indicators, although rarely defined according to human rights principles or standards.

Although the OHCHR indicators mark significant progress in defining global human rights indicators in normative terms and in terms of compliance, a number of challenges remain. The first is the question of how to apply methodologies such as the OHCHR indicators *in practice* and how to promote interpretative consistency. However, such guidance may not resolve a second critical issue, which relates to the dearth of specific data

Table 3.2. Identifying Human Rights Indicators at Different Levels of Development Practice

Indicator Initiative	Level	Category	Measurement tools
OHCHR Indicators for monitoring compliance with international human rights instruments	Global	Compliance assessment (positive approach)	Structural, process and outcome indicators based on various sources. Comparison not intended, except possibly over time
CIRI Human Rights Data Project	Global	Compliance assessment (negative approach, violations-based)	Scores based on expert assessment. Comparative measures
Monitoring the Millennium Development Goals	Global	Performance assessment	Bench-marking targets. Comparative
American Bar Association Judicial Reform Index	Regional: emerging and transitional countries	Compliance with perceived standards	Qualitative expert assessment based on perceived justice sector standards
European Inclusion Index	Regional	Performance assessment of laws and policies	Expert-based scoring. Comparative
Human rights compliance assessment, Danish Institute for Human Rights	Sector-based	Compliance assessments by private sector actors	Online self-assessment by private actors as regards a business-relevant translation of human rights standards
DFID: A Practical Guide to Assessing and Monitoring Human Rights in Country Programs	Program indicators	Performance assessments	Country offices to set benchmarks and indicators
Save the Children: Getting It Right for Children	Program indicators	Performance assessment	Indicators relating to livelihood, participation, policies, equity and nondiscrimination, and civil society capacity

Source: The authors.

and evidence in a number of countries, especially in developing countries where statistical capacity may be low.

In addition, there are other challenges faced in attempts to use human rights indicators in development programming at country and local levels.

- First, how to link performance at the micro-level to that at the macro-level. An alternative and perhaps more fruitful approach might be to concentrate on whether tangible change has occurred at each level and then to seek to understand the causal mechanisms at those distinct levels rather than attempt to link them.
- Second, how to use cross-cutting indicators, i.e., the use of indicators in programs that are also used at the macro and middle levels by the OHCHR, or in relation to the Millennium Development Goals. Such indicators can be used at the outcome

level, but they can also relate to human rights principles. Such indicators may be able to make use of data that are available at the local level—for instance, in respect of health and education. The use of cross-cutting indicators may also facilitate understandings of standards and the effectiveness of particular instruments to generate impact.

■   Third, how to ensure the effective use of benchmarks and targets at the programming level. Such measures may provide precision, but they may sometimes be overly output-oriented and convey little about substantive changes in the enjoyment of human rights or the quality of processes, outcomes, and stakeholder commitment related to human rights realization.

Notes

1. OECD/DAC, 2002. *Glossary of Key Terms in Evaluation and Results Based Management, Evaluation and Aid Effectiveness*, (Development Assistance Committee). 25, Danida, 2006. *Monitoring at Programme and Project Level – General Issues*, Technical note, 3–5. See also www.oecd.org/dac/evaluation.

2. Quoted in Joanne Abbot and Irene Gujit, 1998. *"Changing Views on Change: Participatory Approaches to Monitoring the Environment,"* International Institute for Environment and Development, SARL Discussion Paper 254, 40.

3. Maria Green, 1999. What *We Talk about When We Talk about Indicators: Current Approaches to Human Rights Measurement*, (UNDP ,International Anti-Poverty Law Center, New York).

4. Marike Radstaake and Daan Bronkhorst, 2002. *Matching Practice with Principles. Human Rights Impact Assessment: EU Opportunities*, (Utrecht, HOM) 2, and "Appendix 2: The Use of Indicators." 47–48.

5. Erik André Andersen and Hans-Otto Sano, 2006. *Human Rights Indicators at Programme and Project Level. Guidelines for Defining Indicators, Monitoring and Evaluation.* (Copenhagen, Danish Institute for Human Rights) 11. OECD, Development Assistance Committee defines indicators as "Indicator: Quantitative or qualitative factor or variable that provides a simple and reliable means to measure achievement, to reflect the changes connected to an intervention, or to help assess the performance of a development actor."

6. See www.metagora.org. http://www.portal-stat.admin.ch/iaos2000/01iaos.htm.

7. UNDP, 2005. *Governance Indicators. A User's Guide.* (Oslo, UNDP).

8. OHCHR. The Guidelines were finally published in 2006 under the title *Principles and Guidelines for a Human Rights Approach to Poverty Reduction Strategies.* http://www.ohchr.org/Documents/Publications/PovertyStrategiesen.pdf (2006).

9. http://www.oecd.org/department/0,3355,en_2649_15577209_1_1_1_1_1,00.html.

10. http://www.undp.org/mdg/tracking_targetlist.shtml.

11. For an overview of data sources, see also UNDP, 2006. *Indicators for Human Rights Based Approaches to Development. A Users' Guide.*

12. This has been part of the endeavor of the Metagora program; see *supra n.* 61.

13. Fukuda-Parr, Saikiko, 2006. *Millennium Development Goal 8: Indicators for International Human Rights Obligations. Human Rights Quarterly,* Vol. 28, 966–997.

14. See Malhotra, Rajeev, and Nicholas Fasel, 2005. *Quantitative Human Rights Indicators. A Survey of Major Initiatives.* Draft Paper presented at an Expert Meeting on Human Rights Indicators in Åbo/Turku, Finland, March 11–13, 2005.

15. See *supra n.* 61 at 3.

16. See e.g., Metagora, 2006. *Measuring Human Rights and Democratic Governance to Inform Key Policies.* Advanced Draft. (OECD) 65–66. See also Todd Landman, 2004. *Measuring Human Rights: Principle, Practice, and Policy. Human Rights Quarterly,* Vol. 26, 906–31.

17. See Judith Ducek, Manuel Guzman, and Bert Verstappen, 2001. *Huridocs Events Standard Formats. Documenting Human Rights Violations.* 2nd revised ed. (Huridocs).

18. Todd Landman and Julia Häusermann, 2003. *Map-Making and Analysis of the Main International Initiatives on Developing Indicators of Democracy and Good Governance.*(Ipswich, University of Essex, Human Rights Center.) 21. Also Fons Coomans, Fred Grünfeld, and Menno T. Kamminga (Eds.), 2009. *Methods of Human Rights Research.* Maastricht Centre for Human Rights. Intersentia.

[19] Sakiko Fukuda-Parr, 2001. *Indicators of Human Development and Human Rights Statistical* in *Journal of the United Nationals Economic Commission for Europe*, Vol. 18, No. 2,3, 2001. 244.

[20] See Appendix A for treaty bodies monitoring and enforcing provisions of core human rights treaties.

[21] See the background paper for the exercise: Rajeev Malhotra and Nicholas Fasel, 2005. *Quantitative Human Rights Indicators. A Survey of Major Initiatives*. OHCHR. The final report for the first round of work was published in May 2006; see Fifth Inter-Committee Meeting of the Human Rights Treaty Bodies, 2006. *Report on Indicators for Monitoring Compliance with International Human Rights Instruments*. HRI/MC/2006/7. May 11. The second round of indicator development was completed in June 2008, summarized in Seventh Inter-Committee Meeting of the Treaty Bodies, June 23–25, 2008: *Report on Indicators for Promoting and Monitoring the Implementation of Human Rights*. HRI.MC. 2008.3. June 6, 2008. http://www2.ohchr.org/english/issues/indicators/documents.htm

[22] In Appendix B, the attributes defined as regards the right to food are illustrated.

[23] .See Rajeev Malhotra and Nicholas Fasel, 2006. *Quantitative Indicators for Monitoring the Implementation of Human Rights. A Conceptual and Methodological Framework*. Background Paper. March 24, 2006. See also the final report, Fifth Inter-Committee Meeting of the Human Rights Treaty Bodies, 2006. *Report on Indicators for Monitoring Compliance with International Human Rights Instruments*. HRI/MC/20006/7.

[24] Appendix B illustrates the different types of indicators in the context of the right to food.

[25] The distinction between obligations of result and of conduct derives from the International Law Commission and has been further elaborated by the Committee on Economic, Social and Cultural Rights in its interpretation of article 2.1 of the covenant on progressive realization of economic, social, and cultural rights. See Margot Salomon with Arjun Sengupta, 2003. *The Right to Development: Obligations of States and the Rights of Minorities and Indigenous Peoples*. Minority Rights Group International. Issues Paper. See also the following quote from the Maastricht Guidelines on Violations of ESCR: "The obligations to respect, protect and fulfil each contain elements of obligation of conduct and obligation of result. The obligation of conduct requires actions reasonably calculated to realise the enjoyment of a particular rights. In the case of the right to health, for example, the obligation of conduct would involve the adoption and implementation of a plan of action to reduce maternal mortality. The obligation of result requires States to achieve specific targets to satisfy a detailed substantive standard. With respect to the right to health, for example, the obligation of result requires the reduction of maternal mortality to levels agreed at the 1994 Cairo International Conference on Population and Development and the 1995 Beijing Fourth World Conference on Women." See Theo van Boven, Cees Flinterman, and Ingrid van Westendorp, 1998. *The Maastricht Guidelines on Violations of Economic, Social and Cultural Rights*. SIM Special No. 20 (Utrecht, Netherlands Institute of Human Rights).

[26] The obligation to respect requires states to refrain from interfering with the enjoyment of rights. The obligation to protect requires states to prevent violations of rights by third parties. The obligation to fulfil requires states to take appropriate legislative, administrative, budgetary, judicial, and other measures toward the full realization of such rights. See *Ibid*.

[27] See Hans-Otto Sano, 2007. *Implementing Human Rights. What Kind of Record?* In Rikke Frank Jørgensen and Klaus Slavensky (Eds.) *Implementing Human Rights. Essays in Honour of Morten Kjærum*. (Copenhagen, The Danish Institute for Human Rights) 107–125.

[28] The rights covered include, for example, the right to food, the right to the highest attainable standard of physical and mental health, the right to life, the right to judicial review of detention, the right to education, the right to adequate housing, the right to participate in public affairs, the right not to be subject to torture, the right to fair trial, the right to work, the right to freedom of opinion and expression, and the right to social security. The social right indicators include the use of MDG indicators in a number of instances.

[29] The high-level task force on the implementation of the right to development was established by the Commission on Human Rights, in its resolution 2004/7, and the Economic and Social Council, by its decision 2004/249, at the recommendation and within the framework of the Working Group, in order to assist it in fulfilling its mandate. Para. 2. http://www2.ohchr.org/english/issues/development/right/high_level_task_force_Right_to_Development.htm

[30] Promotion and Protection of All Human Rights, Civil, Political, Economic, Social, and Cultural Rights, including the Right to Development Report of the working group on the right

to development on its 10th session* (Geneva, June 22–26, 2009) Chairperson-Rapporteur: Arjun Sengupta. A/HRC/12/28.

[31] Report of the high-level task force on the implementation of the right to development on its sixth session (Geneva, January 14–22, 2010). Addendum, *Right to development criteria and operational sub-criteria* A/HRC/15/WG.2/TF/2/Add.2 (10 March 2010).

[32] See *supra* n. 79.

[33] The 2005 volume was titled *European Civic and Inclusion Index*, 2005. Research Designed and Co-ordinated by Professor Andrew Geddes and Jan Niessen. Compiled by Laura Citron and Richard Gowan. (Brussels British Council). The 2007 work had the following reference: Niessen, Jan, Thomas Huddleston, and Laura Citron in cooperation with Andrew Geddes and Dirk Jacobs, 2007. *Migrant Integration Policy Index.* Migrant Policy Group. (British Council and EU INTI Programs).

CHAPTER 4

Integrating Human Rights into Development: Indicator Implications

Introduction:
Levels and Degrees of Convergence

Having explored the nature of the convergence between human rights and development and introduced the field of human rights indicators, this chapter describes in conceptual terms the levels at which the convergence can be identified, in order to chart with greater precision how human rights are integrated into development and what role human rights indicators play in this process. The discussion also identifies relevant human rights indicators and their use in development practice at three distinct levels.

The connections between human rights and development are identifiable at three distinct but interrelated levels: dimensions, principles, and obligations.[1] The process of integrating human rights into development activities can take many forms and be based upon quite different rationales, and this discussion draws inspiration from the framework developed by Piron and O'Neil.[2] Three different approaches are identified as important: (1) human rights dimensions in development are linked to *nonexplicit* and nonsystematic approaches; (2) integration of human rights principles is a more systematic form of integration, but it also a moderate one that allows overlaps with more general development concerns; and (3) mainstreaming of human rights obligations is a more formal way, linked to rights-based approaches.[3]

In commenting on the trend during the last decade, the Development Assistance Committee of OECD (DAC) stated recently:

> A decade ago, the DAC affirmed, with High Level Meeting endorsement, the promotion of human rights as an essential part of development co-operation. Since that time, human rights and development have been converging. Not only is there growing recognition of the crucial links between human rights violations, poverty, exclusion, vulnerability and conflict, there is also increasing acknowledgement of the vital role human rights play in mobilizing social change; transforming state-society relations; removing the barriers faced by the poor in accessing services; and providing the basis for the integrity of information services and justice systems needed for the emergence of dynamic market-based economies. This has led many OECD DAC Members and multilateral donors to look at human rights more thoroughly as a means for improving the quality of development co-operation. Many development agencies have adopted policies incorporating human rights and put these into practices.[4]

Many OECD DAC Members and multilateral donors now view human rights as a means for improving the quality of development cooperation, and several development agencies have adopted policies incorporating human rights and put these into practice.

A Framework Outlining the Modes of Integration

Development and human rights occupy many of the same spheres. At a first level, this substantive overlap relates simply to the shared areas of activity, where the expanding remit of development activities (connected also with the broadening understanding of development) map increasingly with areas covered by provisions of human rights treaties and instruments.

Although this convergence relates only to the substantive overlap of development and human rights activities and remains largely coincidental, one may characterize such development activities as possessing human rights *dimensions*. In this sense, human rights emerge in substantive or notional ways, through identifiable similarities or affinities between human rights and the coverage of development activities. The level of integration of human rights in development activities often remains, however, unsystematic and rarely explicit. The *nonexplicit* integration of human rights in development programs is exemplified in programs that may relate to human rights subject matter but may not use human rights language (e.g., programs on health and education) or may do so only selectively or occasionally (e.g., the rights of workers or children). Such integration of human rights is not connected to duties on states or other actors and does not include reference to international human rights treaties or standards of any sort. Thus, these are development activities that share common features or dimensions with human rights, or may resemble human rights in some ways, but that are not conceived in human rights terms and do not have the fulfilment or protection of human rights as their objectives.

At a second level, convergence is discernable at the level of common *principles*. This represents a second, more deliberate form of *rapprochement* around key organizing principles and signaling a more concerted integration of human rights into development. At this level, the convergence relates to the *more* systematic integration of human rights *principles*, such as equality and nondiscrimination, participation and inclusion, accountability and the rule of law, into development programs. There is an identifiable convergence around *principles* such as accountability[5] and participation,[6] the principles of equity and inclusion, and the concept of good governance[7] as a prerequisite for sustainable development.[8] At this level, the relevance or affinity of human rights to development is stronger, involving greater engagement at a normative level. Human rights principles may act as a guide and baseline for development activities and for rights-based programs, both in terms of process as well as outcomes, such as is evident in the "mainstreaming of HR principles."

At a third level, there is the convergence around the area of human rights *obligations*, which lie at the heart of the human rights framework, because all rights imply correlative duties. It is here that the most explicit approaches to human rights can be identified and where human rights–based approaches to development are clearly discernable. At this level, the notion of human rights is directly connected with the legal obligations of both donors and recipients and may be identified in states and non-state actors, linking the processes and outcomes of development with human rights obligations. It requires that development activities enhance and support the realization of rights and that development activities are not undermining the enjoyment of rights. At the programming level, such an approach views development cooperation through the lens of human rights obligations and may lead to the grounding of development projects and programs in explicit human rights language.

These different modes of integration are outlined in table 4.1, which highlights how the existing government and donor practices can be seen as a graduated approach to human rights integration in development. The OECD DAC study also offers a concise description of the different modes of integration of human rights and development, which have been mapped to the typology of this work in the following (box 4.1).

Human Rights Indicators at Three Levels of Convergence of Human Rights and Development

If human rights are understood to be relevant to development at any of the levels identified, human rights indicators have a necessary relevance as well: there is no way to dissociate

Table 4.1. Three Modes of Human Rights Integration

	Human Rights Dimensions	Human Rights Principles	Human Rights Obligations
Nonexplicit Integration	Substantive overlap between the areas covered by human rights and development. Largely coincidental, and integration is not systematic. No explicit commitment to human rights. Program goals rarely based on human rights, occasional reliance on human rights indicators.		
Integrating Human Rights Principles		Strategic and sectoral integration of human rights principles, such as participation, inclusion, nondiscrimination, "do no harm." Program goals may include human rights but are also informed by other perspectives or driven by other principles.	
Integrating human rights accountability			Legal accountability emphasized, focus on duty-bearer conduct acknowledging rights-based approaches. Explicit groundings of programs in human rights norms and obligations and rights language.

Source: The authors.

Box 4.1. OECD Description of the Approaches of Donor Agencies

"Some agencies are not explicitly using a human rights framework at a policy level, but aspects of their policies and programming are consistent with what explicit human rights approaches would call for, such as a focus on empowerment and inclusion. . . . Many donor agencies have adopted gender equality policies that call for both gender mainstreaming and interventions specifically targeted at gender equality" (corresponding to what is termed a nonexplicit approach in this introduction).

"An increased number of donor agencies support human rights as part of a broader governance agenda. Governance has become a priority in donor policies and programmes because it lies at the heart of national development strategies. . . . Many agencies seek to mainstream human rights as a cross-cutting issue in development assistance, beyond the direct support to human rights programmes and stand-alone projects that support human rights organizations" (Ibid., pp. 10–11) (illustrative of approaches integrating human rights principles).

OECD reports: "Some agencies are implementing some form of a "human Rights-based approach". These approaches vary, but usually feature the integration of human rights principles –such as participation, inclusion and accountability—into policies and programmes. They also draw on specific human rights standards—such as freedom of expression and assembly – to help define development objectives and focus programmatic action" (Ibid. p. 11) (illustrative of approaches integrating human rights accountability).

Source: OECD DAC, 2007. Action-Oriented Policy Paper on Human Rights and Development. OECD.

the relevance of human rights from human rights indicators. Nowhere is this more evident than in development. In formal terms, human rights indicators are an essential part of substantiating and implementing human rights legal standards and principles and, to that extent, are linked with the introduction of a measure of accountability by providing standards against which to assess development activities and progress.

In this way, they provide the specific means through which to assess both processes and outcomes in the development context. In terms of substance, human rights indicators emanate from the international human rights standards and the international human rights framework, which are underpinned by the principles of equality and nondiscrimination, accountability, voice and participation, and equity. Substantively, therefore, human rights indicators advance those principles and are permeated by them. The following discussion traces human rights indicators at three levels of convergence.

Dimensions: Substantive Overlap

At a practical and substantive level, human rights and development appear to share common or at least complementary goals, and, in this realm, the spheres of influence of development and human rights are overlapping. This is the level at which there exist synergies in substance but where there is no express linkage at the level of principle or legal obligation: this overlap is widely discussed in academic literature.[9] Human rights are directly relevant to the goals of poverty reduction, reducing inequity and inequality, and promoting good governance—such that certain development goals or activities enjoy human rights dimensions. Such common goals are sometimes fortuitous, but they may nevertheless result in positive reinforcement.

An illustrative example of human rights dimensions in development can be found in the MDGs. Although the eight Millennium Development Goals[10] established in the Declaration of the United Nations General Assembly 2000 were not formulated in a human rights language, the Declaration itself firmly anchored the key objectives of the international community—including the MDGs—within the international legal framework of human rights and human rights principles.[11] There is, moreover, strong overlap between human rights as goals and the MDGs themselves.

Human rights indicators relating to the right to life, the right to education, the rights of women, and the highest attainable standard of health may overlap with or be similar to specific targets and indicators of MDGs goals of poverty and hunger eradication, education, gender equality, health, and HIV/AIDS. In other words, in terms of operational agendas, human rights and MDG realization have strong affinities and similarities.[12] The same data sets are relevant. Although they are not cast in terms of obligation, a key *implication* of the MDG agenda and focus is to strengthen international community accountability to substantive social norms, goals, and targets. The MDGs bring some measure of accountability for substantive social and human development targets, although that accountability would be strengthened by some legal and normative anchorage for the achievement of the specific outcomes relevant to each goal that the human rights framework offers.

Most social sector programs employ indicators that have no explicit human rights content. Indicators are formulated by reference to the MDGs or to broader development objectives. Human rights issues may be integrated, but it is not done consistently or systematically.[13] Human rights indicators that emerge at this level may include outcome indicators related to vulnerable groups or occasional references to women's rights and reproductive health rights or to rights of children.

At this level, human rights–related indicators emerge primarily as outcomes indicators, i.e., as part of indicators reflecting results of programs in terms of actual enjoyment of rights or development achievements by social groups or individuals, although they may also be manifest in process indicators related to participation and consultation.

Table 4.2. Nonexplicit Human Rights Integration: The Human Rights Dimensions of Development

Description	Examples drawn from development policy and practice	Human rights indicators of primary relevance
A human development approach in which the human person is defined as both the subject and the object of development typically overlaps with human rights. Activities in areas such as health and education or concerning specific groups, such as women, indigenous peoples, or children, likewise yield overlaps.	Sector programs and projects in which service delivery (food, health, education, housing, or water) are substantial issues. Policies: Cross-cutting dimensions: gender and democratization, and issue-based social policies, e.g., workers' rights.	*Outcome indicators:* Little reliance on human rights indicators. Development indicators are prevalent, some of which incorporate human rights dimensions and resemble human rights outcome indicators. *Examples:* MDG indicators overlap with specific human rights process and outcome indicators, but the rights reference of MDG monitoring is nonexistent; Poverty reduction strategies have sometimes included rights and rights-related indicators, but they do so only occasionally and with respect to social outcomes related to vulnerable groups.[14]

Source: The authors.

This type of reliance on human rights indicators is characteristic of international development agencies and development banks, which adopt a *nonexplicit* approach to the integration of human rights. Under such approaches, there are few if any references to rights in official policies or project documents, and approaches are not human rights–based in any systematic manner, which explains the limited human rights content of indicators used and the limited occurrence of human rights indicators themselves. This helps illustrate how activities set forth as human rights–*promoting* in development activities are, in fact, more appropriately understood as human rights-*related*. Vulnerability of particular groups, such as indigenous women or children, is not approached directly and explicitly through the lens of nondiscrimination.[15] The application of human rights indicators at this level occurs as an indirect consequence of their inclusion in the broader pool of development indicators and human development indicators. A more systematic approach to the integration of human rights might sharpen the focus of the relevant indicators and introduce a stronger emphasis on empowerment and on disaggregation between groups. As illustrated in table 4.2, a nonexplicit integration of human rights leads to the possible incorporation of certain outcome indicators, but has limited scope for assessing whether or how duty-bearers design policies out of broader human rights concerns.

Integration of Human Rights Principles

At a second level, there is an identifiable convergence around principles, such as accountability[16] and participation,[17] equality and nondiscrimination and equity,[18] inclusion, empowerment, transparency, and principles related to good governance[19] as a prerequisite for sustainable development.[20] Among these, principles that focus on *process* are of particular importance,[21] and therefore the human rights indicators that feature most prominently are process-based human rights indicators. At this level, human rights principles are explicitly

Table 4.3. Mainstreaming Human Rights Principles

Description	Examples drawn from development policy and practice	Human rights indicators of primary relevance
▩ Human rights principles included in the U.N. Common Understanding of the Implementation of a Human Rights–Based Approach to Development, established in Stamford in 2003: ▩ Universality and inalienability; indivisibility ▩ Interdependence and interrelatedness ▩ Equality and nondiscrimination ▩ Participation and inclusion ▩ Accountability ▩ Rule of law, and access to justice Principles with a particular importance for programming include ▩ Equality and nondiscrimination ▩ Participation ▩ Inclusion ▩ Accountability ▩ Rule of law ▩ Access to justice	▩ The World Bank Operational Policy on Indigenous Peoples OP (4.20) and on Environmental Assessment OP (4.01) applies principles of participation, consultation, and inclusion; OP 4.20 also mentions the human rights of indigenous peoples. ▩ Donor gender mainstreaming often refers to principles of nondiscrimination, participation, and inclusion. Danida 2006 Performance Report comments on gender as a cross-cutting dimension. ▩ Accra Agenda for Action, paragraphs 3 and 13 (c)	▩ *Process indicators* in respect of donor efforts to mainstream human rights principles are indicators of primary relevance, especially in relation to inclusive and participatory processes of consultation. Other indicators may have relevance: ▩ *Outcome indicators* disaggregated by gender. ▩ Examples: Percentage of core funds dedicated to gender issues. OECD. Regular gender audits, including baseline data and monitoring. OECD. Number of complaints received by national human rights institutions and by ombudsman's institutions on human rights. OHCHR. Proportion of voting age population registered to vote. OHCHR. Proportion of students starting grade 1 who reach grade 5 disaggregated by sex. OHCHR. Worldwide Governance Indicators on the Rules of Law.

Sources: OECD, DAC, 2006. *Gender Equality and Aid Delivery: What has Changed in Development Cooperation Agencies since 1999?* OECD. Royal Danish Ministry of Foreign Affairs, 2007. *Annual Performance Report 2006.* The U.N. Stamford Declaration on a Human Rights-Based Approach, See U.N. Development Group, 2003: *The Human Rights Approach to Development Cooperation. Towards a Common Understanding among the U.N. Agencies.* See www.undg.org/documents. World Bank Institute, 2007. *Governance Matters,* see http://info. worldbank.org/governance/wgi2007/. OHCHR 2007. *Indicators for Monitoring Compliance with International Human Rights Instruments. Third Expert Consultation, Geneva, 19–20 December 2006. Draft Conclusions and Recommendations.*

and more deliberately integrated in development policy and practice, although their use does not necessarily entail a rights-based approach. Without discounting the important *normative* significance, these principles may also be integrated in development practice for primarily functional reasons.[22] Table 4.3 elaborates on the identification of human rights principles with an operational importance, as detailed by the 2003 U.N. Common Understanding on a Human Rights–Based Approach to Development Cooperation. The second column of the table provides examples of government and donor practices. As the third column explains, examples of human rights indicators related to or derived from human rights principles are mostly process indicators, defining how states parties are making efforts to improve equality, participation, and the rule of law. Thus, U.N. agencies, as well as donors, relate human rights support to processes of participation and inclusion, to gender equality, and, in some cases, to nondiscrimination.[23]

Some have argued that the Paris Declaration on Aid Effectiveness may eventually contribute to an increased use of human rights–based indicators as a result of the commitment to performance assessment on alignment of partner government and donor practices, a commitment to harmonization, and a commitment to improve performance on the management of aid for development results.[24]

This may entail the development of stronger methods of monitoring, including assessment of processes of participation.[25] Furthermore, some commentators have opined that the Paris Declaration emphasis on ownership and mutual accountability may support further efforts to mainstream principles of participation and equity, particularly given the increased recognition of the mutual relevance of so-called cross-cutting policy issues—such as gender, human rights, and environment—to aid effectiveness.[26] This compatibility at the level of principle may be due to several factors, such as the evolution of development discourse beyond economic growth to incorporate social and human development, a stronger focus on ownership,[27] inclusion and empowerment and capacity-building,[28] and a deepened recognition of the role of governance and responsive accountable institutions for sustainable development objectives.[29] This potential for convergence at the level of principle may be seen to be further substantiated in the Accra Agenda for Action, which notes (in paragraph 3) respect for human rights as a cornerstone of development.[30] The AAA also cites, in paragraph 13 (c), human rights in its provision for an expanded policy dialogue: "Developing countries and donors will ensure that their respective development policies and programmes are designed and implemented in ways consistent with their agreed international commitments on gender equality, human rights, disability and environmental sustainability."[31] It is noteworthy, however, that the AAA does not include targets or indicators on human rights.

In terms of strategic approach, human rights principles may be viewed by donors as a option for human rights integration that is preferable to that of approaches defined as rights-based approaches, but it is still stronger than those defined here as *nonexplicit* reference. Programming goals might be framed in terms of human rights principles, such as equality and nondiscrimination or attention to vulnerable groups, rather than human rights goals or by reference to substantive human rights. Instruments of implementation may be cast in terms of rights-holder or duty-bearer, but human rights capacity-building may feature on a par with other instruments. Indicators reflect human rights considerations, but they may be combined with indicators that have been informed by other dimensions as well.

The implications for human rights indicators are that greater reliance is likely to be placed on all three types of previously identified indicator, even though the approach is unlikely to be *based* on obligations. In addition, specific indicators of vulnerability, exclusion, and marginalization of groups in relation to social outcomes are more likely to be manifest. The increasing emphasis on good governance, transparency, and accountability may also result in greater use of civil and political rights indicators. The following section explores the integration of human rights principles into the broader development by focusing on the select examples of equity and equality; accountability, and participation—analyzing the human rights indicators at issue for each.

Equity and Equality

Although the concepts of equity and equality are not synonymous, there are ways in which they resemble one another and could be viewed as analogous and complementary notions drawn from development and human rights, respectively. Principles of equality and nondiscrimination are at the foundation of the international human rights framework.[32] They are the source of substantive equality rights, but they are also essential to the full respect, protection, and fulfilment of other human rights.[33] The international human rights framework incorporates a variety of forms of discrimination, including direct and indirect discrimination, as well as private discrimination.[34] Human rights approaches to equality demand that content and consequence of laws be scrutinized, acknowledging that the formal recognition of an "equal capacity" for rights is not enough.

For its part, equity has strong human rights content and is prominent in development discourse. The WDR 2006 on *Equity and Development* defined equity according to two basic principles: equality of opportunity and the avoidance of absolute deprivation. It confirms that inequities have deep impact on development and that structural and systemic inequalities can impede economic growth. It advanced intrinsic and instrumental reasons for addressing inequality and confirmed the scope for redistributive principles and policies, as well as institutional reform aimed at leveling the political and economic playing field. It recognized that inequalities of different types are mutually reinforcing and interdependent, which can result in inequalities replicating over time.[35] Although equity and human rights provisions related to equality and antidiscrimination bear strong affinity, a greater reliance on human rights standards might lend the former greater precision and normative anchorage and provide a baseline against which to assess programs or policies.

The compatibility of the principles of equality and equity has two potential implications for the formulation of indicators: first is a shared emphasis on human rights indicators that target exclusion, discrimination, and inequality in general, whether they are formulated in explicit human rights terms or not. In development discourse, indicators concerned with inequity could be strengthened by references to human rights through a broadened understanding of the concept of vulnerability, which may call for better methods of disaggregation—not only according to gender, but according to age, citizenship, and status and treatment of immigrants.[36] Indicators relating to child rights are increasingly important and provide an additional impetus to the integration of social rights.[37] Human rights indicators related to equality tend to focus more naturally and clearly on the most excluded and vulnerable. Second, they bring with them a strong normative content and specific legal baselines and standards against which to assess performance. For instance, the existing measurement of gender-related development and of gender empowerment undertaken by the UNDP (gender-related development index and gender empowerment measures) are formulated without an emphasis on the rights dimensions of equality or state legislation and policy on rights related to the family, such as marriage, divorce, and inheritance.

Accountability

The principle of accountability defines a fundamental purpose of the human rights framework. Human rights offer groups and individuals a means to hold their governments and others to account under domestic and international law. Human rights make duties owed by governments to their people a matter of international concern through enshrining duties that correlate with rights in treaties to which states subscribe in signature and ratification. Accountability results from the enforcement of duty. Rights offer a means of enforcing that duty. Effective accountability is viewed by some as the single most important contribution that human rights can make to improve development, particularly as it pertains to process and obligations of effort on the part of states.

Accountability is relevant to development at several levels and in relation to different development policy objectives and activities. It is prominent in the 2005 Paris Declaration principle of mutual accountability, and its emphasis on accountability mechanisms and adequate monitoring of reciprocal commitments to enhance aid effectiveness are examples of this.[38] Social accountability is essential to sustainable development and poverty reduction through its emphasis on civic engagement and the involvement of poor people as active agents. The WDR 2004 *Making Services Work for the Poor* highlighted accountability as essential for the attainment of the MDGs and for making services work, which depends not only on economic growth and the flow of resources but on the ability to translate those resources into basic services, especially in health, education, water, and sanitation.[39] Human rights principles are seen to have value in the area of social policy, by helping connect the supply and demand side of governance and the improving the delivery and access to social services, through enhancing monitoring and accountability and ensuring mechanisms of participation and consensus-building in the definition of services and implementation arrangements.[40]

From the private sector perspective, the Equator Principles and corporate social responsibility initiatives[41] in development activities evidence a growing recognition of the need for effective accountability as part of managing risk and fostering sustainable development.[42] Similarly, the U.N. Global Compact calls for the mainstreaming of 10 principles in business activities[43] to promote responsible corporate citizenship so that the private sector can help realize a more sustainable and inclusive global economy. Finally, the IFC's 2006 *Policy on Social and Environmental Sustainability* recognizes that "the roles and responsibility of the private sector in respecting human rights are emerging as an important aspect of corporate social responsibility. The performance standards developed by IFC to help private sector clients address environmental and social risks and opportunities are consistent with these emerging roles and responsibilities."[44] In this connection, it is worth noting that the IFC has, in collaboration with IBLF and UNGC, developed a *Guide to Human Rights Impact Assessment and Management*[45] that is designed to help IFC private sector clients assess the human rights impacts in their investment decisions and operations and make appropriate management decisions. The *Guide* has been subject to road-testing since 2007, and the revised, online version was officially launched during the U.N. Global Compact Leaders Summit in New York on June 25, 2010. The new version of the *Guide* is built on lessons learned from the road-testing process, results of the public consultation process, advice from the External Advisory Panel especially set up around the revision of the *Guide*, and recent policy developments in the business and human rights area.

The principle of accountability relies on indicators that may illustrate acceptance, commitment, and effort of governments and duty-bearers. A number of examples of indicators are illustrative. The acceptance of human rights obligations in the form of adherence to covenants and conventions may be seen as a first step. In development programming, this may translate into an explicit acknowledgment of how specific human rights conventions and standards are important to the field of programming. For instance, in social sector support programs (health, water, and education), program objectives and their adjoining indicators have often been defined without any reference to the rights dimensions of educational reform or of water supply. Within the health sector, the proliferation of programs focusing on HIV/AIDS and the elaboration of global policies with a human rights perspective[46] may have contributed to stronger linkages between health sector objectives and efforts of nondiscrimination and inclusion.

Commitment and effort may be reflected in human rights promotional activities, such as the establishment of ombuds, facilitating human rights monitoring at the domestic level. Another important indicator is the institutionalization of complaints facilities anchored in national institutions or in specific parts of the executive branch. Activities in the area of improving access to information and justice are also important indicators, including those that address local and community dispute resolution mechanisms and those that link formal and informal systems. The Judicial Reform Index, elaborated by the American Bar Association (ABA) and the Central European and Eurasian Law Initiative (CEELI), is an example of indicator efforts in this field (see Appendix C). Indicators revealing enhanced access to information (the right to seek information) point to an enhanced commitment to human rights accountability and of good governance practices, especially in countries where human rights civil society groups are active.[47] The Human Rights Review undertaken by DFID in 2004 stressed a strategic principle defined as "fulfilling obligations" that stated: *"strengthening institutions and policies which ensure that obligations to protect and promote the realisation of rights for all are fulfilled by states and other duty-bearers. Actions to increase directly the public accountability of governments and other duty-bearers."* Among the areas of intervention identified under the heading of "fulfilling obligations" were CSO engagement in treaty monitoring process, national budgets and poverty plans based on human rights obligations, and,police force with capacity to respect and protect human rights and act as a service to the community.[48]

Participation

Participation is a key operative principle of the human rights framework and pervades it at several levels.[49] It is the foundation of several core human rights recognized for intrinsic worth,[50] but it is also understood as having an accessory character and as being instrumentally relevant to the fulfilment of other rights.[51] Conversely, participation itself depends on other rights, such as freedom of expression and the right to information.[52]

Participation ensures that development strategies respond to actual priorities and needs of poor people and helps promote the sustainability and legitimacy of development activities. It is fundamental to the empowerment of poor people and marginalized groups and enables dialogue with those in power.[53] Participation is widely viewed as a fundamental component of good development practice: it pervades Poverty Reduction Strategies[54] and is enshrined in aspects of development policies, such as the World Bank safeguard policies governing investment projects.[55] In this way, participation illustrates some convergence of development policy and practice and human rights at the level of principle.[56]

When the Office of the High Commissioner for Human Rights established indicators measuring the right to participate in public affairs during 2006 to 2007, "the proportion of voting-age population registered to vote" was among the process indicators identified (see table 4.3). However, like most human rights indicators related to participation, this indicator tends to link participation to elections, when a broader array of participation-related human rights indicators exist, and this is particularly evident in relation to development activities. Indicators relating to the human rights principle of participation can capture its organizational and institutional aspects (such as the processes of participation in defining goals and programs such as the PRS), processes of advocacy and empowerment (dialogues, collaborative activism, and community participation of specific groups), and legal outcomes, e.g., "the establishment of laws allowing the flourishing of an independent civil society."[57] In the DFID Human Rights Review 2004, a number of possible interventions are mentioned in the field of participation and inclusion. Examples include decentralization, which successfully increases participation of marginalized people, and access to information to combat corruption through local citizens monitoring of government action

The foregoing discussion illustrates the synergies and complementarities between the principles operative in development and human rights. There are, nevertheless, a number of differences. Divergences exist between the analogous principles emerging in development and human rights practices (e.g., equity and equality). For instance, gender empowerment is often conceived without incorporating its rights dimensions with the consequences that indicators of women's empowerment tend to become indicators of social development—without insufficient attention to violence against women or to the relevance family law. Second, there may be tensions between interpretations of the same principles. Third, several core human rights principles do not have corresponding analogues in development (e.g., indivisibility, universality, and inalienability of human rights.). The foregoing illustrates some of the potential contributions of human rights to analogous development principles and how indicators drawn from human rights principles may facilitate specification and concretization.

Obligations

Development and human rights can be seen to intersect around legal obligations, albeit implicitly. Even though international legal obligations are relevant to both development and human rights, they do not feature prominently in development discourse, and indeed the idea of development assistance, defined in terms of obligations, remains controversial.[58] To the extent that human rights and development overlap and human rights are incorporated into development discourse, the notion of obligations needs to be addressed explicitly because human rights imply duties,[59] "rights require correlative duties,"[60] and without duty there is no right.[61] These basic points tend not to be reflected in development policy, and efforts to consolidate good development practice related to human rights, without connecting it to duty, may arguably lead to confusion. Similarly, efforts to integrate human rights in development without the systematic integration of human rights indicators may result in inconsistent and weak baselines for assessing development processes and outcomes.

Despite the substantive relevance of several human rights treaties to development, it is in the realm of obligations that the tensions between development and human rights discourse may be most evident. Human rights *obligations* have no established place in development policy and practice, and indeed the discourses associated with each exemplify the divergences between human rights and development. Moreover, development approaches have sometimes been argued to run counter to basic human rights obligations: examples include user fees for primary education or the privatization of water. Finally, the notion of legal obligation drawn from treaties is less used in development policy, which tends to be cast in terms of more loosely aligned, nonbinding goals and targets and organized around programs, strategies, and approaches.

At this level, therefore, human rights can be understood as the subjects of voluntarily undertaken obligations under international human rights treaties to which states are party. Viewed in this way, human rights are thus the subjects of international legal obligation that states are bound to uphold in a variety of contexts, including when they participate in international development. Greater clarity on this may help advance an understanding of the role that development policy and institutions may play in supporting countries' efforts to fulfill those obligations. Exploring this dimension may help promote greater policy coherence at the international level[62] and focus attention on existing duties, modalities, and processes to uphold human rights in development rather than by highlighting the putative human rights obligations of non-state actors.

Table 4.4 contains examples of indicators relevant to the level of obligations. The Cingranelli and Richards human rights database, which has broad country and chronological coverage, is based on violations and focused on civil and political rights, but with some reference to social rights. CIRI indicators are primarily outcome indicators of respect for human rights, inasmuch as they indicate the actual enjoyment of rights by citizens in a given country. The Human Rights Compliance Assessment elaborated by the Human Rights and Business Department of the Danish Institute for Human Rights is an online tool for assessing how corporations can become accountable for human rights. The indicators for monitoring the Millennium Development Goals are of increasingly relevance because the recent definition of human rights compliance indicators by OHCHR employs the MDG indicators as process as well as outcome indicators.

Table 4.4 illustrates how donors, international organizations, and state as well as non-state actors have strengthened policies that enhance human rights obligations and accountability of these actors, including through the use of human rights indicators. However, it is important to underline that governments, international agencies, and NGOs have been reluctant so far to employ systematic and global indicators when measuring human rights accountability, presumably, at least in part, because of the political sensitivity involved. Thus, in the practices of state and international actors, there is no discernable uniformity in measuring human rights accountability, although the use of OHCHR compliance indicators in duty-bearer reporting to treaty bodies may help promote a more systematic approach to accountability measurement. A number of other challenges persist

Table 4.4. Assessing Human Rights Obligations

Description	Examples drawn from development policy and practice	Human rights indicators of primary relevance and examples
▥ Activites are based on or focus on relevant human rights treaty obligations ratified by a country. ▥ This requires (1) duty-bearers accepting human rights obligations, (2) that they undertake efforts to fulfil these in terms of legal, institutional, and resource-allocating strategies. Duty-bearers enter into dialogue with rights-holders ▥ Ultimately, these measures of accountability and empowerment result in outcomes improving the actual enjoyment of human rights.	▥ Sweden's *Shared responsibility—Sweden's policy for global development*—acknowledging a rights perspective as one pillar and linking this not only to development assistance. ▥ UNICEF and UNDP adopting rights-based programming as a guiding principle for activities. This implies, e.g., advocacy, support for legislation, monitoring, and civil society rights–based cooperation. ▥ E.U. Commission: protection of human rights is one of the cornerstones of the policy in third countries. ▥ Systematizing human rights expectations in connection with U.N. peacekeeping operations ▥ The agreement by a number of larger business corporations under the Global Compact that they will not be complicit in human rights violations.	▥ *Structure, process. and outcome indicators* related to state obligations to respect, protect, and fulfil within their own territories, as well as those indicating support of human rights activities by state and private actors in other territories ▥ Example of indicators: ▥ Cingranelli-Richards Human Rights Database: indicates human rights violations of civil, political, economic. and social rights by state actors. ▥ OHCHR indicators so far based on eight civil, political, economic and social rights. Indicators measuring acceptance, efforts, and outcomes of state/duty-bearer laws and policies. ▥ The Human Rights Compliance Assessment (HRCA): an online indicator tool, allowing companies to run a 360° check of human rights risks in the company or project.

Sources: See Government Offices of Sweden, updated 2007. *Shared Responsibility—Sweden's Policy for Global Development.* http://www.sweden.gov.se/sb/d/3102;jsessionid=aYYdMG4jcq_h. EU Commission, External Relations, Updated 2006. *Promotion of Human Rights and Democratisation in the European Union's External Relations. http://www.consilium.europa.eu/showPage.aspx?id=1634&lang=en.* United Nations, 2003. *Handbook on UN Multidimensional Peacekeeping Operations.* Cingranelli-Richards (CIRI) Human Rights Database. See www.humanrightsdata.com. OHCHR indicators, see *supra* note 58. U.N. Stats, 2007: *Millennium Development Goals Indicators.* The Human Rights Compliance Assessment of the Danish Institute for Human Rights, see http://www.humanrightsbusiness.org/.

in respect of the human rights accountability of duty-bearers: these include those related to the putative obligations of non-state actors, the legal obligations of state actors when they act as donors or as members of international organizations, or the differences in the nature of obligations for economic, social, and cultural rights (as opposed to civil and political rights).[63] Each of these sets of challenges impacts the formulation of indicators in this field.

Figure 4.1 provides examples of how human rights indicators may vary, depending on whether they relate to states' efforts to fulfil their own human rights obligations (all states) or whether they operate in the capacity as donors and lenders supporting other governments to fulfil human rights obligations.

At the structural level, human rights indicators refer to the formal legal framework of rights and accession to human rights treaties, by which states create for themselves human rights obligations and join the framework of the international human rights regime. Indicators applicable to all states (left side of figure 4.1) may inform on the question of

Figure 4.1. Fulfilling Human Rights Obligations of Developing States and of States Acting as Donors: Human Rights Activities (A) and Indicators (I)

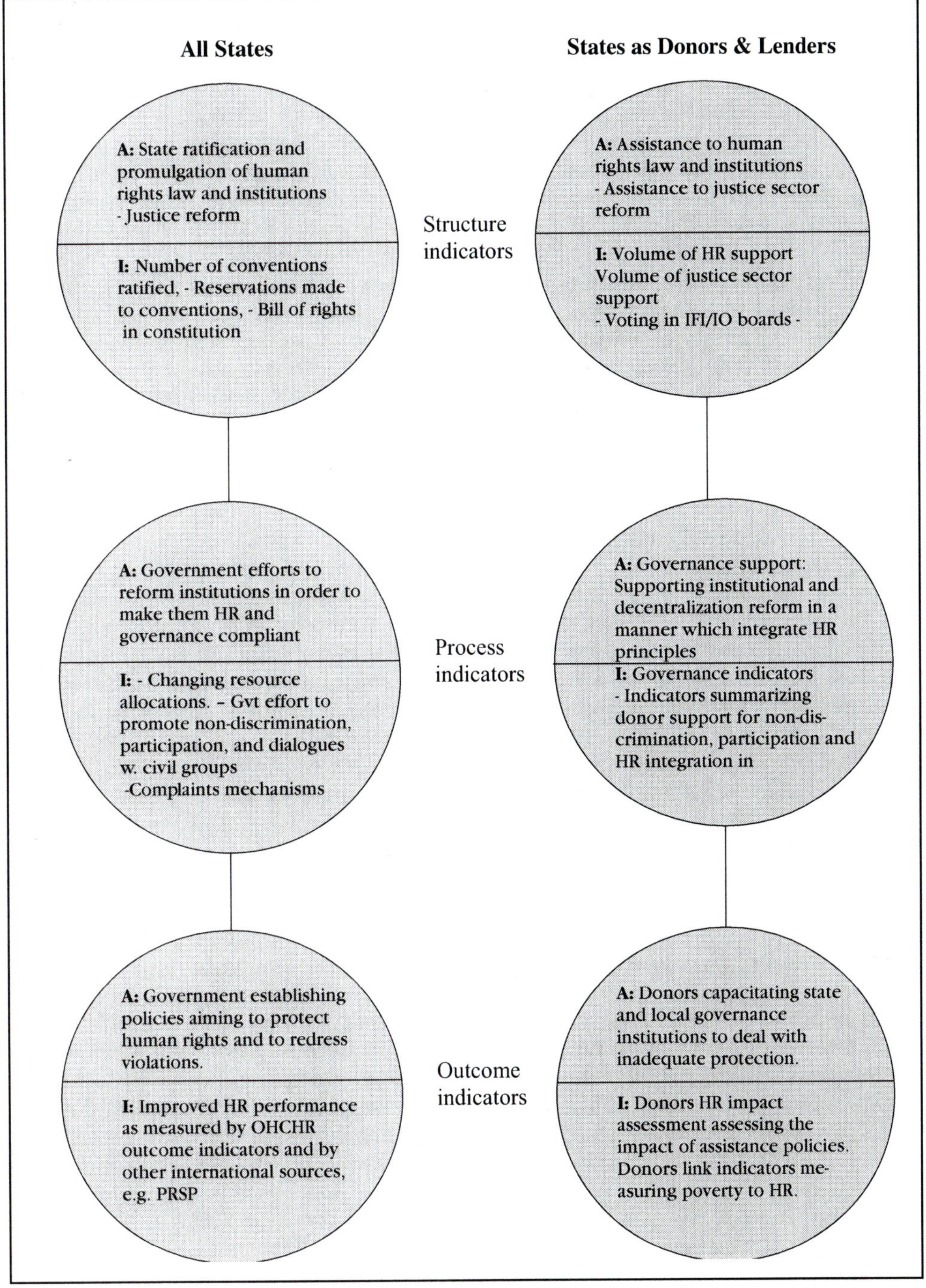

All States

States as Donors & Lenders

A: State ratification and promulgation of human rights law and institutions
- Justice reform

I: Number of conventions ratified, - Reservations made to conventions, - Bill of rights in constitution

A: Assistance to human rights law and institutions
- Assistance to justice sector reform

I: Volume of HR support Volume of justice sector support
- Voting in IFI/IO boards -

Structure indicators

A: Government efforts to reform institutions in order to make them HR and governance compliant

I: - Changing resource allocations. – Gvt effort to promote non-discrimination, participation, and dialogues w. civil groups
-Complaints mechanisms

A: Governance support: Supporting institutional and decentralization reform in a manner which integrate HR principles
I: Governance indicators
- Indicators summarizing donor support for non-discrimination, participation and HR integration in

Process indicators

A: Government establishing policies aiming to protect human rights and to redress violations.

I: Improved HR performance as measured by OHCHR outcome indicators and by other international sources, e.g. PRSP

A: Donors capacitating state and local governance institutions to deal with inadequate protection.

I: Donors HR impact assessment assessing the impact of assistance policies. Donors link indicators measuring poverty to HR.

Outcome indicators

formal legal acts in relation to international instruments, on the passing of laws relevant to rights, or the existence of bills of rights in the constitutions. Indicators related to states as donors or lenders (right side of the figure) may reveal the level of support for the human rights in *other* countries, including efforts of international cooperation on human rights.

At the process level, the indicators applicable to all states (left side of figure 4.1) capture government activities related to reforming institutional behavior, including efforts to decentralize resource allocation and decision making. These indicators may illustrate evolving priorities and commitments through changing resource allocations or through the promotion of policies and institutional reform which ensure nondiscrimination, participation, interaction with civil societies, and the institutionalization of complaints mechanisms. In respect of states as donors or lenders (right side of figure 4.1), indicators may reflect support for governance or may reveal efforts to promote human rights principles and the integration of human rights in decentralization policies.

At the outcome level, indicators measure how states seek to redress human rights violations, and they act to harmonize donor contributions in fields that may impact human rights, as well as how donors support efforts to deal with inadequate human rights protection or fulfilment in developing countries. Outcome indicators applicable to all states are those identified as outcome indicators by OHCHR, and these relate generally to the enjoyment of rights under U.N. human rights treaties to which those states are party. Outcome indicators applicable to donors may relate to upholding the principle of "do no harm" in development cooperation, which may be implemented through human rights impact assessments. However, it should be underlined that the foregoing reflects a potential theoretical framework for such indicators rather than an account of their use in practice.

The employment of human rights indicators is indicative of an approach in which governments, operating within their own territories or in their capacity as donors, assume responsibility in accordance with their international human rights obligations. Such strategies are illustrated by rights-based approaches, although very few donors self-consciously characterize their development cooperation strategies as explicitly and directly rights-based,[64] and even fewer link such strategies directly to human rights obligations. In the absence of such a general commitment and given the range of existing approaches, it may be argued that the use of human rights–based indicators becomes all the more important for donors and lenders, particularly at the outcome level, which measures changes in actual human rights enjoyment. The reliance on human rights indicators emanating from international human rights treaties might serve to promote coherence and consistency at the international level and further donor harmonization in relevant fields.

This chapter has outlined three modes of integrating human rights into development: a *non-explicit* approach, integrating human rights principles, and integrating human rights obligations. The chapter has attempted to connect the various modes of human rights integration with various types of human rights indicators. Consistent with OHCHR practice, this analysis distinguishes between structure, process, and outcome indicators. Only under a human rights obligations approach analyzed in chapter 3 are all the three levels of human rights indicators included as a practice, whereas the *non-explicit* approach to integration typically only relates to human rights in select references to actual enjoyment of rights (outcomes) and the occasional incorporation of principles, such as participation or equality and equity. With human rights obligations vested in states as the primary duty-bearers, it may be useful to consider and distinguish how states use human rights indicators generally and how they use them as donors. There is a growing interest in documenting how donors and lenders fulfil their human rights obligations—but also in ascertaining how donors and lenders support borrowing or recipient states' fulfilment of similar obligations and how to determine whether development assistance undermines human rights enjoyment.

Notes

[1] This basic approach and typology is relied upon in Siobhán McInerney-Lankford, 2007, *Development and Human Rights: Some Institutional Perspectives* (2007) Netherlands Quarterly of Human Rights, Vol. 25 (3). 459–504

[2] Laure-Hélène Piron, with Tammie O'Neil, 2005, conducted an extensive review of the subject, focusing on HRBA, HR mainstreaming, HR, Dialogues, HR projects, and Implicit HR work. See *Integrating Human Rights into Development. A Synthesis of Donor Approaches and Experiences.* (Overseas Development Institute, September 2005).

[3] OECD DAC, 2006. *Integrating Human Rights into Development: A Synthesis of Donor Approaches, Experiences and Challenges* (OECD DAC). 27, Table 1.

[4] OECD DAC 2007. See *supra* n. 16.

[5] Thus, the HDR 2000 demonstrated how the human rights framework brings principles of accountability and social justice to the process of human development. It also argues for a more integrated view of human rights and human development

[6] On the centrality of participation to RBA to development, the OHCHR makes the following observation, "Rights-based approaches require a high degree of participation, including from communities, civil society, minorities, indigenous peoples, women and others. According to the UN Declaration on the Right to Development, such participation must be "active, free and meaningful" so that mere formal or "ceremonial" contacts with beneficiaries are not sufficient." http://www.unhchr.ch/development/approaches-04.html. See also A. Frankovits and P. Earle, 1996, (3rd ed., 2001)., *The Rights Way to Development: A Human Rights Approach to Development Assistance* (Marrickwill, The Human Rights Council of Australia) 117.

[7] "Good governance is indispensable to the realization of human rights in general [...]." B. Hamm, 2001. *A Human Rights Approach to Development* in *Human Rights Quarterly.* Vol. 23, 4.

[8] World Bank, Governance: The World Bank's Experience, 1994; I .F. I. Shihata, *"Issues of "Governance"* in The World Bank Legal Papers, 2000. 245, 271–272; Daniel Kaufmann, Aart Kraay, and Massimo Mastruzzi: *Governance Matters IV: New Data and New Challenges.* (World Bank).

[9] See especially articles by Philip Alston, 2005; Mac Darrow and Amparo Tomas, 2005; Sano, 2000. See also Piron, Laure-Hélène, and Francis Watkins, 2004. *DFID Human Rights Review. A Review of How DFID Has Integrated Human Rights in Its Work.* (Overseas Development Institute, July 2004).

[10] The goals are (1) eradicating extreme poverty and hunger; (2) achieving universal primary education; (3) promoting gender equality and empowering women; (4) reducing child mortality; (5), improving maternal health; (6) combatting HIV/AIDS, malaria, and other diseases; (7) ensuring environmental sustainability; and (8) developing global partnerships for development. See http://www.undp.org/mdg/

[11] Philip Alston, 2005. See *supra* n. 17 at 756.

[12] See *supra n.* 61; United Nations, 2002, developed indicators, several of which were similar to the targets under the MDGs.

[13] It is interesting to see how and how much the human rights agenda influences new joint strategies of assistance under the Paris Declaration. The Ghana Growth and Poverty Reduction Strategy (GPRS II) elaborated under the Joint Assistance Strategy emanating from the Paris agenda of Aid Effectiveness, Harmonization and Alignment, features the human rights theme as a means to stronger governance. Human rights are also related to the protection of women and children and to the protection of vulnerable groups. Government of the Republic of Ghana, 2007. Ghana Joint Assistance Strategy (G-Jas). Commitment by Partners to Work towards GPRS-II Goals and Harmonization Principles. During 2003, the DG Development of the European Commission issued a guide for monitoring progress in the education sector. Although the report underlined equity as a major theme—and with that the importance of disaggregation according to gender—it contained no reference to human rights. See European Commission, DG Development, Development Policy and Sectoral Issues, 2003. *Tools for Monitoring Progress in the Education Sector.* During 2006, DFID's Health Resource Centre made an Assessment of the Impact of Global Health Partnerships. Country Case Study Report (India, Sierra Leone, and Uganda). In this study, the indicators discussed are development indicators. Human rights references can be found in one of the country appendices and in the footnotes, but they are not informing any of the assessment methodologies.

[14] PRSPs reveal sporadic and inconsistent references to rights. See for instance Tanzania's PRS from June 2005. United Republic of Tanzania, Vice President's Office, 2005. *National Strategy for Growth and Reduction of Poverty* (NSGRP). In this document, there are operational targets for Child Protection

and Rights (with respect to child labor), whereas health, water, and education services are not linked to social rights. See at 48. In the Bangladesh PRS of 2005, a strategic goal of Women's Advancement and Rights is defined, but all other social sector issues are referred to without reference to a rights discourse. See General Economics division, Planning Commission, Government of People's Republic of Bangladesh, 2005. *Unlocking the Potential. National Strategy for Accelerated Poverty Reduction.* (Bangladesh).

[15] See *supra* n. 77.

[16] Thus, the HDR 2000 demonstrated how the human rights framework brings principles of accountability and social justice to the process of human development. It also argues for a more integrated view of human rights and human development.

[17] On the centrality of participation to RBA to development, the OHCHR makes the following observation, "Rights-based approaches require a high degree of participation, including from communities, civil society, minorities, indigenous peoples, women and others. According to the UN Declaration on the Right to Development, such participation must be "active, free and meaningful" so that mere formal or "ceremonial" contacts with beneficiaries are not sufficient." http://www .unhchr.ch/development/approaches-04.html. See also A. Frankovits and P. Earle, 1996 (3rd ed., 2001). See *supra* n. 13 at 117.

[18] WDR, 2006. *Equity and Development*, see also *supra* n. 14.

[19] "Good governance is indispensable to the realization of human rights in general [...]." Brigitte Hamm, 2001. *A Human Rights Approach to Development. In Human Rights Quarterly.* Vol. 23. 4.

[20] See *supra* n. 90, D. Kaufmann, A. Kraay, and M. Mastruzzi: *Governance Matters IV: New Data and New Challenges.* (The World Bank Institute).

[21] For reference to the latter, see Report: *Second Interagency Workshop on Implementing a Human Rights–Based Approach in the Context of the UN Reform*, 2003. 6. See *supra* n. 23.

[22] Mac Darrow and Amparo Tomas, 2005. *Power, Capture, and Conflict: A Call for Human Rights Accountability in Development Cooperation* in *Human Rights Quarterly*, Vol. 27, 501.

[23] This was evident in the donor presentations of human rights–based policies at a workshop held in Copenhagen during 2006. Although Department for International Development (DFID) emphasize participation and inclusion, which is coupled to notions of social protection, the Swedish SIDA emphasize similar principles, but also nondiscrimination, accountability, and transparency.

[24] See Workshop on Development Effectiveness in Practice. *Applying the Paris Declaration to Advancing Gender Equality, Environmental Sustainability and Human Rights.* Workshop hosted by Irish Aid, organized jointly by the Development Assistance Committee's Networks on Environment and Development, Governance, and Gender Equality and the Working Party on Aid Effectiveness Funded by the Governments of Ireland and Denmark, 2007.

[25] See OECD, DAC, 2007. *Working Party on Aid Effectiveness and Donor Practices.* Concept Note for the Dublin Workshop April 26–27, 2007, 4.

[26] Marta Foresti, 2006. *Human Rights and Paris Declaration.* ODI OECD DAC HRTT *Human Rights and Aid Effectiveness* available at OECD website. Papers from Dublin workshop (2007); Dublin +1 Workshop hosted by DFID (2008). OECD DAC Human Rights Task Team, Human Rights and Aid Effectiveness DAC Update (2007); Human Rights and Aid Effectiveness: Key Actions to Improve Inter-Linkages (2008).

[27] OECD 2008. *Better Aid. 2008 Survey on Monitoring the Paris Declaration. Making Aid More Effective by 2010.*

[28] See *supra* n. 8

[29] Patricia Cornwall and John Gaventa, 2001. Highlight the principles of accountability and participation as key to improving governance.

[30] Gender equality, respect for human rights, and environmental sustainability are cornerstones for achieving enduring impact on the lives and potential of poor women, men, and children. It is vital that all our policies address these issues in a more systematic and coherent way.

[31] http://siteresources.worldbank.org/ACCRAEXT/Resources/4700790-1217425866038/AAA-4 -SEPTEMBER-FINAL-16h00.pdf. Examples of such agreed commitments include international human rights treaty obligations entered into by states parties.

[32] Wouter Vandenhole, 2005. *Non-Discrimination and Equality in the View of the UN Human Rights Treaty Bodies.* (Antwerp/Oxford Intersentia).

[33] Paul Sieghart, 1983. *The International Law of Human Rights* (Oxford, Clarendon Press)17–18.

[34] For a comprehensive discussion of international law provisions on equality and protection against discrimination, see Warwick McKean, 1983. *Equality and Discrimination under International Law.* (Oxford: Clarendon Press) For a comprehensive work on comparative perspectives, see T.

Loenen and P. Rodrigues (eds.), 1999. *Non-Discrimination Law: Comparative Perspectives*, in The Hague: Kluwer Law International. For a discussion of the European human rights context, see Oddny Mjoll Arnardóttir, 2002. *Equality and Non-Discrimination under the European Convention on Human Rights*.(Martinus Nijhoff, Brill), and of particular relevance in this context is the expansion effected by Protocol 12 of the ECHR, which modifies the accessory character of the ECHR equality provision, rendering it free standing rather than applicable only in relation to or in conjunction with substantive provisions of the Convention: See Jeroen Schokkenbroek, *A New Standard against Discrimination*: Negotiating Protocol No 12 to the European Convention on Human Rights in Jan Niessen and Isabelle Chopin (Eds.), 2004, *The Development of Legal Instruments to Combat Racism in a Diverse Europe*, (Martinus Nijhoff, Brill), 61.

[35] WDR, 2006, and on the potential negative consequences of inequality traps (e.g., crime and violence) 51. For other research in this vein, Frances Stewart, 2005. *Policies towards Horizontal Inequalities in Post-Conflict Reconstruction*, CRISE Working Paper No. 7, March 2005, 49 (CRISE, Queen Elizabeth House, Oxford University) http://www.crise.ox.ac.uk/pubs/workingpaper7.pdf.

[36] See for instance Jan Niessen et al. 2007. Migrant Integration Policy Index (MIPEX), *supra n.* 89.

[37] See Save the Children, 2007, *Getting It Right for Children. A Practitioner's Guide for Child Rights Programming*. (London, Save The Children).

[38] For the full text of the Paris Declaration on Aid Effectiveness (2005), see http://www.oecd. org/dataoecd/11/41/34428351.pdf. However, according to observers of the process, the mutual accountability part remains one of the dimensions least described under the Paris Declaration. So far, it does not *seem* to have had any impact on how the donors deal with human rights indicators.

[39] http://econ.worldbank.org/WBSITE/EXTERNAL/EXTDEC/EXTRESEARCH/EXTWDRS/EXTWDR2 004/0,,menuPK:477704~pagePK:64167702~piPK:64167676~theSitePK:477688,00.html.

[40] World Bank, 2007, *Realizing Rights through Social Guarantees*. Report 40047-GBL.

[41] E.g., Business Leaders Initiative on Human Rights; Danish Institute's Human Rights Compliance Assessment Tool

[42] See e.g., A. Vies, 2004. *The Role of Multilateral Development Institutions in Fostering Corporate Social Responsibility*, 47(3) in Development (Inter-American Development Bank). Vol. 47, 45–52.

[43] http://www.unglobalcompact.org/AboutTheGC/index.html. **Human Rights**. Principle 1: businesses should support and respect the protection of internationally proclaimed human rights. Principle 2: make sure that they are not complicit in human rights abuses. **Labor Standards.** Principle 3: Businesses should uphold the freedom of association and the effective recognition of the right to collective bargaining. Principle 4: the elimination of all forms of forced and compulsory labor. Principle 5: the effective abolition of child labor. Principle 6: the elimination of discrimination in respect of employment and occupation. **Environment**. Principle 7: businesses should support a precautionary approach to environmental challenges. Principle 8: undertake initiatives to promote greater environmental responsibility. Principle 9: encourage the development and diffusion of environmentally friendly technologies. **Anti-Corruption**. Principle 10: businesses should work against all forms of corruption, including extortion and bribery.

[44] http://www.ifc.org/ifcext/enviro.nsf/Content/EnvSocStandards.

[45] For more information, see www.guidetohria.org.

[46] UNAIDS, Office of the High Commissioner for Human Rights, 2006. *International Guidelines on HIV/AIDS and Human Rights*. Consolidated Version. (Geneva).

[47] Field work in India during September 2007 showed that duty-bearers considered The Freedom of Information Act as one of the most important instruments in making themselves more accountable.

[48] Laure-Hélène Piron and Francis Watkins, 2004. See *supra* n. 91.

[49] Henry Steiner, 1988, *Political Participation as a Human Right*, in Human Rights Yearbook, 77, Lisa VeneKlasen, Valerie Miller, Cindy Clark, and Molly Reilly, 2004, *Rights-Based Approaches and Beyond: Challenges of Linking Rights and Participation*. In IDS Working Paper no. 235.

[50] Foremost among these is the right to participate in the conduct of public affairs and in particular the right to take part in the government of one's country directly or through freely chosen representatives (UDHR Article 21) or to take part in the conduct of public affairs, directly or through freely chosen representatives, and to vote (Article 25 ICCPR).

[51] E.g., the right to equal access to public service in his country (Article 21 (2)). Moreover, the duties that individuals owe to their communities cannot be fairly or properly imposed if the correlative rights to participate in those communities are not respected (Article 29, UDHR).

[52] E.g., freedom of thought and conscience (Article 18, UDHR), the right to freedom of expression (Article 19) or the right to education (Article 26).

[53] Lisa VeneKlasen et al., see *supra n.* 106.

[54] Acknowledging this as a matter of principle or policy is not intended to discount the problems attendant to participation, in particular, how to ensure the quality, breadth, and thoroughness of the participation: who participates, how they participate, and in relation to what can or will they participate. See F. Stewart and M. Wang, 2005. *"PRSPs within the Human Rights Perspective"* in Mary Robinson and Philip Alston, 2005. *Human Rights and Development: Towards Mutual Reinforcement,* (Oxford, OUP). See *supra n.* 22. 454.

[55] Participation is an explicit requirement of World Bank policy O.P. 4.20 Indigenous Peoples and inheres in a number of other safeguard policies' consultation requirements, including that contained in O.P. 4.20, Indigenous Peoples; O.P. 4.01 Environmental Assessment; OP /BP 4.04 Natural Habitats; OP 4.09 Pest Management O.P./ B.P. 4.12 Involuntary Resettlement; OP/BP 4.36 Forests; OPN 11.03 Cultural Property.

[56] Celestine Nyamu and Andrea Cornwall, November 2004. *What Is the "Rights-Based Approach" All About?* See *supra n.* 45 Perspectives from the International Development Agencies in IDS Working Paper 234, Laure-Hélène Piron and Francis Watkins, 2004. See *supra* n. 91: "Some of the operational implications of a human rights-based approach are similar to the key elements of 'good development practice, such as ensuring wide stakeholder participation," at 10.

[57] See for instance the section on participation in OHCHR 2003, *Draft Guidelines: A Human Rights Approach to Poverty Reduction Strategies.*

[58] See e.g., Sigrun Skogly, 2006. *Beyond National Borders: States' Human Rights Obligations in International Cooperation.* (Intersentia).

[59] See discussion *supra* and *infra,* and *see* generally J. Waldron (ed.), 1984, *Theories of Rights,* (Oxford, OUP).

[60] Asbjørn Eide, 2001. *Economic, Social and Cultural Rights as Human Rights* in Asbjørn Eide, Catarina Krause, and Allan Rosas, 2001. *Economic, Social and Cultural Rights: A Textbook* (Dordrecht, Martinus, Nijhoff). 22.

[61] On the relationship between rights and duties or duty-bearers and right-bearers, see "choice" theory of rights (e.g., Herbert Hart) and "benefit" or "interest" theories of rights, which focus on duty (e.g., Bentham, Raz, Lyons, McCormick). On the "correlativity of rights and duties," Bernard Mayo, *What Are Human Rights?* in D. D. Raphael (ed.), 1967, *Political Theory and the Rights of Man,* (Indiana UP) 68,72.

[62] Margot E. Solomon, 2007. See *supra n.* 49.

[63] See Margot E. Salomon, Arne Tostensen, and Wouter Vandenhole, 2007, *Human Rights, Development and New Duty-bearers.* In: *Casting the Net Wider: Human Rights, Development and New Duty-Bearers.* (Antwerp, Intersentia) 3–17. See also *supra n.* 52.

[64] E.g., Sida, the Swedish International Development Cooperation Agency promotes "a human rights perspective" rather than a human rights–based approach. See DFID's How to Note, 2009. *A Practical Guide to Assessing and Monitoring Human Rights in Country Programmes.*

CHAPTER 5

Conclusions

The discussion in previous chapters has set forth perspectives on the nature of the overlap between human rights and development and outlined approaches to that overlap. It has also analyzed the convergence of human rights and development, the roles and justifications for integrating human rights into development, as well as the tensions that persist between the discourses. Given the potential relevance of human rights for development, the chapters have outlined the role and relevance of human rights *indicators* for development in intrinsic and instrumental terms, particularly in how they may connect the normative core of human rights standards and principles with empirical data of various sorts.

Indicators are used at different levels for different purposes, e.g., to measure the current situation in a given country or to measure the impact and performance of a particular program so that a wide range of measures, methodologies, and uses can be identified. Two principal methodologies of indicator formulations can be identified in human rights assessment: (1) compliance indicators measuring the human rights accountability of primary states as duty-bearers (including as donors), and (2) indicators measuring the effectiveness of program implementation. Positive rather than negative assessment is also discernable in relation to the duty-bearer accountability of states, with monitoring institutions reluctant to focus on a systematic assessment of human rights violations, seeking instead to use softer language in indicators focused more on progressive realization. At the program and project levels, variations in context and purpose render efforts to streamline indicators across localities, regions, countries, and continents very challenging—even when the basic methodology is uniform (e.g., PRS). Ambitions to create common human rights indicators from the micro- to the macro-levels have rarely been realized. Even with a common conceptual approach, the contexts of development localities and institutions vary immensely, making such efforts difficult.

A distinct trend is evident in relation to state duty-bearers as donors. There is little consistency about the level and modalities of human rights support across the donor community. Human rights dimensions of general assistance policies are acknowledged in some areas and sectors but not in others. The mainstreaming of human rights principles is largely implicit and unsystematic, and human rights accountability is often unclear when human rights are integrated in governance strategies without the corresponding rights-specific indicators. Moreover, the place of human rights obligations in this context remains unclear. Donor coordination and strategies on harmonization, consistency, and joint methodologies already place some reliance on indicators, which may open the possibility of use of human rights indicators in future should those activities expand to cover human rights explicitly. Similarly, should the understanding of the core Paris Declaration principles of mutual accountability, ownership, harmonization, and alignment and managing for results evolve to rely on human rights frameworks, relevance on human rights indicators might become more obvious. This report has aimed to contribute to the discourse on human rights and development by elucidating the possible modes for approaches to the integration of human rights in development and setting forth the relevance of human rights indicators to each of these. It does not endorse any particular approach to either the process of human integration or the use of human rights indicators, but it merely posits that human rights indicators are an essential element of any incorporation of human rights into development, whether at the *nonexplicit* level of development activities that have a human rights dimension, or through the integration of human rights principles to approaches based directly on human rights obligations.

Nevertheless, the report illustrates how existing approaches to human rights indicators in development remain inchoate, with rationales rarely explicit and application unsystematic. Regardless of the approach employed for the integration of human rights in development and notwithstanding the appropriateness of more limited approaches in certain institutional settings, establishing clear and consistent rationales for the use of human rights indicators in development policy and activities may contribute greater coherence to the understanding of the role of human rights in development more generally.

CHAPTER 6

Literature Review

Books, Articles and Published Reports

Abbot, Joanne and Irene Gujit, 1998. *"Changing Views On Change: Participatory Approaches to Monitoring the Environment,"* International Institute for Environment and Development, SARL Discussion Paper 254.

Alston, Philip, 2005. *"Ships Passing in the Night: The Current State of the Human Rights and Development Debate Seen through the Lens of the Millennium Development Goals,"* Human Rights Quarterly, Vol. 27, 3.

Alston, Philip and Mary Robinson, 2005. (Eds.). *Human Rights and Development: Towards Mutual Reinforcement.* (Oxford, OUP).

Andersen, Erik André and Hans-Otto Sano, 2006. *Human Rights Indicators at Programme and Project Level. Guidelines for Defining Indicators, Monitoring and Evaluation.* (Copenhagen, Danish Institute for Human Rights).

Arnardóttir, Oddny Mjol, 2002. *Equality. and Non-Discrimination under the European Convention on Human Rights.* (Martinus Nijhoff, Brill).

Bartels, Lorand, 2005. *Human Rights Conditionality in the EU's International Agreements.* (Oxford, OUP).

Bell, Daniel A. and Jean-Marc Coicaud, 2006. *Ethics in Action. The Ethical Challenges of Human Rights-Nongovernmental Organizations.* (Cambridge, Cambridge University Press and United Nations University).

van Boven, Theo, Cees Flinterman, and Ingrid van Westendorp, 1998. *The Maastricht Guidelines on Violations of Economic, Social and Cultural Rights. SIM Special No. 20* (Utrecht, Netherlands Institute of Human Rights).

Brownlie, Ian, 2003. *Principles of Public International Law. 6th edition* (Oxford, OUP).

Clapham, Andrew, 2006. *Human Rights Obligations of Non-State Actors.* (Oxford, OUP).

Coomans, Fons, Fred Grünfeld, and Menno T. Kamminga (Eds.), 2009. *Methods of Human Rights Research.* Maastricht Centre for Human Rights.(Antwerpen, Intersentia).

Cornwall, Patricia, and John Gaventa, 2001. *Participation in Governance* in Huque, A.S., and Zafarullah, H. (Eds.), International Development Governance. (London, Taylor and Francis).

Cranston, Maurice, 1973. *What Are Human Rights?* (New York, Taplinger Publishing Co.).

Daňino, Roberto, 2005. "Legal Aspects of the World Bank's Work on Human Rights: Some Preliminary Thoughts" in Mary Robinson and Philip Alston (Eds.), *Human Rights and Development: Towards Mutual Reinforcement.* (Oxford, OUP).

Darrow, Mac, and Amparo Thomas, 2005. *Power, Capture, and Conflict: A Call for Human Rights Accountability in Development Cooperation* in Human Rights Law Quarterly, Vol. 27, 2.

Decker, Klaus, Siobhán McInerney-Lankford, and Caroline Sage, 2006. *Human Rights and Equitable Development: "Ideals," Issues and Implications.* Background paper to the World Development Report 2006 available at: Permanent URL for this page: http://go.worldbank.org/3AN4HQ0SC0.

DFID's Health Resource Centre, 2006. *Assessing the Impact of Global Health Partnerships. Country Case Study Report (India, Sierra Leone, and Uganda).* (London, GHP Study Paper 7).

DFID, OECD, 2008. Workshop on: *Strengthening the Development Results and Impacts of the Paris Declaration on Aid Effectiveness through Work on Gender Equality, Social Exclusion and Human Rights.* (London, DFID).

DFID, 2009. *A Practical Guide to Assessing and Monitoring Human Rights in Country Programmes.* How To Note. (London, DFID).

Donnelly, Jack, 1985. *The Concept of Human Rights.* (London, Croom Helm).

Donnelly, Jack, 1993. *International Human Rights.* (Boulder, Westview Press).

Donnelly, Jack, 2003. *Universal Human Rights in Theory and Practice,* 2d ed.(Ithaca, Cornell University Press).

Dueck, Judith, Manuel Guzman, and Bert Verstappen, 2001. *Huridocs Events Verjoix Standard Formats. Documenting Human Rights Violations.* Second Revised Edition (Huridocs).

Eide, Asbjørn, 2001. *Economic, Social and Cultural Rights as Human Rights* in Asbjørn Eide, Catarina Krause, and Allan Rosas, 2001. *Economic, Social and Cultural Rights: A Textbook* (Dordrecht, Martinus, Nijhoff).

European Commission, DG Development, Development Policy and Sectoral Issues, 2003. *Tools for Monitoring Progress in the Education Sector.* (Brussels, EME-Office).

European Commission, External Relations, 2007. *Furthering Human Rights and Democracy across the Globe.* (Bruxelles and Luxembourg).

European Commission, External Relations, updated 2006. *Promotion of Human Rights and Democratisation in the European Union's External Relations.* http://ec.europa.eu/external_relations/human_rights/intro/index.htm#1.

Fifth Inter-Committee Meeting of the Human Rights Treaty Bodies, 2006. *Report on Indicators for Monitoring Compliance with International Human Rights Instruments.* HRI/MC/2006/7. (Geneva, U.N.)

Foresti, Martha, David Booth, and Tammie O'Neil, 2006. *Aid Effectiveness and Human Rights: Strengthening the Implementation of the Paris Declaration.* (London, Overseas Development Institute).

Forsythe, David P., 2000. *Human Rights in International Relations.* (Cambridge, Cambridge University Press).

Frankovits, André and Patrick Earle, 2001. *The Rights Way to Development. A Human Rights Approach to Development Assistance. Policy and Practice.* (Marrickvill, The Human Rights Council of Australia).

Fukuda-Parr, Sakiko, 2001. *Indicators of Human Development and Human Rights Statistical* in Journal of the United Nationals Economic Commission for Europe, Vol. 18, 2,3.

Fukuda-Parr, Saikiko, 2006. *Millennium Development Goal 8: Indicators for International Human Rights Obligations.* Human Rights Quarterly, Vol. 28, 4.

Green, Maria, 1999. *What We Talk about When We Talk about Indicators: Current Approaches to Human Rights Measurement.* (UNDP International Anti-Poverty Law Center, New York).

Gready, Paul, 2009. *Reasons to Be Cautious about Evidence and Evaluation: Rights-Based Approaches to Development and the Emerging Culture of Evaluation.* Journal of Human Rights Practice, 1 3.

Gauri, Varun, 2004. *Social and Economic Rights: Claims to Health Care and Education in Developing Countries.* World Development, Vol. 32, 3.

Gauri, Varun and Daniel M. Brinks (Eds.), 2008. *Social and Economic Rights in Developing Countries. Politics, Law and Impact.* (Cambridge, Cambridge University Press).

General Economics Division, Planning Commission, Government of People's Republic of Bangladesh, 2005. IMF Country Report. *Unlocking the Potential. National Strategy for Accelerated Poverty Reduction.* (Bangladesh PRS). (IMF Country Report 05/410).

Government of the Republic of Ghana, 2007. *Ghana Joint Assistance Strategy (G-Jas). Commitment by Partners to Work towards GPRS-II Goals and Harmonization Principles.* February.

Hamm, Brigitte I., 2001. *A Human Rights Approach to Development* in Human Rights Quarterly, Vol. 23, 4.

Hannum, Hurst, 1996. *The Status of the Universal Declaration of Human Rights in National and International Law,* Georgia Journal of International and Comparative Law, Vol. 25.

Henkin, Louis, 1981. *Introduction* in Henkin, Louis (Ed.) *The International Bill of Rights. The Covenant of Civil and Political Rights.* (New York, Columbia University Press).

Henkin, Louis, 1990. *The Age of Rights.* (New York, Columbia University Press).

Jennings, Robert and Arthur Watts, 1992. *Oppenheim's International Law. Volume I: Peace.* (London, Longman).

Kaufman, Daniel, 2005. *Human Rights and Governance: The Empirical Challenge'* in Philip Alston and Mary Robinson, *Human Rights and Development: Towards Mutual Reinforcement* (Oxford, OUP).

Kaufmann, Daniel, Aart Kraay, and Massimo Mastruzzi, 2005. *Governance Matters IV: New Data and New Challenges.* (Washington, World Bank Institute).

Kjær, Mette and Klavs Kinnerup, 2002. *Good Governance—How Does It Relate to Human Rights.* In: Hans-Otto Sano and Gudmundur Alfredsson (Eds.) *Human Rights and Good Governance. Building Bridges.* (Den Hauge, Martinus Nijhoff, Brill).

Lagoutte, Stéphanie, Hans-Otto Sano, and Peter Scharff Smith, 2007. *Human Rights in Turmoil. Facing Threats, Consolidating Achievements.* (Den Hauge, Martinus Nijhoff).

Landman, Todd and Julia Häusermann, 2003. *Map-Making and Analysis of the Main International Initiatives on Developing Indicators of Democracy and Good Governance.* (University of Essex, Human Rights Center).

Landman, Todd, 2004. *Measuring Human Rights: Principle, Practice, and Policy.* Human Rights Quarterly, Vol. 26, 4.

Loenen, T. and P. Rodrigues (Eds.), 1999. *Non-Discrimination Law: Comparative Perspectives.* (The Hague, Kluwer Law International).

Malhotra, Rajeev and Nicholas Fasel, 2005. *Quantitative Human Rights Indicators. A Survey of Major Initiatives.* Draft Paper presented at an Expert Meeting on Human Rights Indicators in Åbo/Turku, Finland. (Geneva).

Malhotra, Rajeev and Nicholas Fasel, 2005. *Quantitative Human Rights Indicators. A Survey of Major Initiatives.* OHCHR. (Geneva).

Malhotra, Rajeev and Nicholas Fasel, 2006. *Quantitative Indicators for Monitoring the Implementation of Human Rights. A Conceptual and Methodological Framework.* Background Paper March 24, 2006. (Geneva).

Mayo, Bernhard, 1967. *What Are Human Rights?'* in D. D. Raphael (Ed.), 1967, *Political Theory and the Rights of Man,* (Bloomington, Indiana UP)

McInerney-Lankford, Siobhán, 2007. *Development and Human Rights: Some Institutional Perspectives* (2007). Netherlands Quarterly of Human Rights, Vol. 25, 3.

McInerney-Lankford, Siobhán, 2009 *Human Rights and Development: A Comment on Challenges and Opportunities from a Legal Perspective.* Journal of Human Rights Practice Vol. 1, 1, 51–82.

McKean, Warwick, 1983. *Equality and Discrimination under International Law.* (Oxford, Clarendon Press).

Meron, Theodore, 1986. *On a Hierarchy of International Human Rights, Discussing the Hierarchical Terminology in International Human Rights.* American Journal of International Law, Vol. 80.

Niessen, Jan, Thomas Huddleston, and Laura Citron in cooperation with Andrew Geddes and Dirk Jacobs, 2007. *Migrant Integration Policy Index.* Migrant Policy Group. (British Council and EU INTI Programs). (Brussels).

Nowak, Manfred, 2002. *A Human Rights Approach to Poverty* in Human Rights in Development Yearbook. *Empowerment, Participation, Accountability and Non-Discrimination* (Eds.) Martin Scheinin and Markku Suksi 2005. (Leiden Martinus Nijhoff Publishers).

Nyamu-Musembi, Celestine, and Andrea Cornwall, 2004. *What Is the "Rights-Based Approach" All About? Perspectives from International Development Agencies.* IDS Working Paper No 234 (Brighton, IDS).

OECD/DAC, 2002. *Glossary of Key Terms in Evaluation and Results-Based Management, Evaluation and Aid Effectiveness.* (Development Assistance Committee).

OECD, DAC, 2006. *Gender Equality and Aid Delivery: What Has Changed in Development Cooperation Agencies Since 1999?* (Paris, OECD).

OECD-DAC, 2006. *Integrating Human Rights into Development. Donor Approaches, Experiences and Challenges.* (Paris, OECD).

OECD, 2007. *DAC Action-Oriented Policy Paper on Human Rights and Development.* (OECD).

OECD DAC Human Rights Task Team, 2007. *Human Rights and Aid Effectiveness: Key Actions to Improve Inter-Linkages.* (Paris, OECD).

OECD, DAC, 2007. *Working Party on Aid Effectiveness and Donor Practices. Concept Note for the Dublin Workshop* April 26–27, 2007, 4. (Paris).

OECD, 2008. *Better Aid. 2008 Survey on Monitoring the Paris Declaration. Making Aid More Effective by 2010.* (Paris and Copenhagen, 2009).

Office of the High Commissioner for Human Rights (OHCHR), 2003. *Draft Guidelines: A Human Rights Approach to Poverty Reduction Strategies.* (Geneva Draft publication written by Paul Hunt, Siddiq Osmani, and Manfred Nowak).

OHCHR, 2006. *Frequently Asked Questions on a Human Rights-Based Approach to Development Cooperation.* (Geneva; New York, United Nations).

OHCHR, 2006. *Principles and Guidelines for a Human Rights Approach to Poverty Reduction Strategies.* (Geneva, OHCHR).

OHCHR, 2007. *Indicators for Monitoring Compliance with International Human Rights Instruments. Third Expert Consultation, Geneva, December 19–20, 2006. Draft Conclusions and Recommendations.*

OHCHR, 2009. *Report of the OHCHR on the Relationship between Climate Change and Human Rights,* U.N. Doc. A/HRC/10/61 (January 15, 2009).

Palacio, Ana, 2006. *The Way Forward: Human Rights and the World Bank* in Development Outreach, October 2006. (Washington, DC, WBI World Bank).

Piron, Laure-Hélène, and Francis Watkins, 2004. *DFID Human Rights Review. A Review of How DFID Has Integrated Human Rights in Its Work.* (Overseas Development Institute, July).

Piron, Laura-Hélène with Tammie O'Neil, 2005. *Integrating Human Rights into Development. A Synthesis of Donor Approaches and Experiences.* (Overseas Development Institute, September 2005). (Paris, OECD).

Radstaake, Marike, and Daan Bronkhorst, 2002. *Matching Practice with Principles. Human Rights Impact Assessment: EU Opportunities.* (Utrecht, HOM).

Regulation (EC) No. 1889/2006 of the European Parliament and of the Council of December 20, 2006 *on Establishing a Financing Instrument for the Promotion of Democracy and Human Rights Worldwide.* Official Journal of the European Union Vol. 29.12.2006 L 386.

Royal Danish Ministry of Foreign Affairs, 2007. *Annual Performance Report 2006.* (Copenhagen, Udenrigsministeriet, Danida).

Seventh Inter-Committee Meeting of the Treaty-Bodies, June 23–25, 2008. *Report on Indicators for Promoting and Monitoring the Implementation of Human Rights.* HRI.MC. June 6, 2008. 3.

Salomon, Margot E. with Arjun Sengupta, 2003. *The Right to Development: Obligations of States and the Rights of Minorities and Indigenous Peoples.* Minority Rights Group International. Issues Paper. (London, MRGI).

Salomon, Margot E. 2007. *International Economic Governance and Human Rights Accountability.* In: M. Salomon, A. Tostensen, and V. Vandenhole (Eds.) *Casting the Net Wider: Human Rights, Development and New Duty-Bearers.* (Antwerp, Intersentia).

Sano, Hans-Otto, 2000. *Development and Human Rights. The Necessary, But Partial Integration of Human Rights and Development.* Human Rights Quarterly, Vol. 22, 3.

Sano, Hans-Otto, 2007. "Does a Human Rights-Based Approach Make a Difference?" In: Margot Salomon, Arne Tostensen, and Wouter Vandenhole, 2007. *Casting the Net Wider: Human Rights, Development and New Duty-Bearers.* (Antwerp, Intersentia).

Sano, Hans-Otto, 2007. *Implementing Human Rights. What Kind of Record?* In: Rikke Frank Jørgensen and Klaus Slavensky (Eds.). *Implementing Human Rights. Essays in Honour of Morten Kjærum.* (Copenhagen, The Danish Institute for Human Rights).

Save the Children, 2007, *Getting It Right for Children. A Practitioner's Guide for Child Rights Programming.* (London, Save The Children).

Schokkenbroek, Jeroen, 2004. *A New Standard against Discrimination*: Negotiating Protocol No. 12 to the European Convention on Human Rights in Jan Niessen and Isabelle Chopin (Eds.), 2004. *The Development of Legal Instruments to Combat Racism in a Diverse Europe.* (Den Hauge, Martinus Nijhoff, Brill).

Sen, Amartya, 1999. *Development as Freedom.* (Oxford, OUP).

Sen, Amartya, 1999. *Democracy as a Universal Value,* in Journal of Democracy, Vol. 10, 3.

Shihata, Ibrahim, 2000. *The World Bank and Human Rights—A Presentation before the 1993 UN World Conference on Human Rights* in The World Bank Legal Papers, 815. (Dordrecht, Martinus Nijhoff Publishers).

Sieghart, Paul, 1983. *The International Law of Human Rights.* (Oxford, Clarendon Press).

Skogly, Sigrun, 2006. *Beyond National Borders*: States' Human Rights Obligations in International Cooperation. (Antwerp, Intersentia).

Skogly, Sigrun I., and Mark Gibney, 2002. *Transnational Human Rights Obligations,* in Human Rights Quarterly, Vol. 24, 3.

Steiner, Henry 1988, *Political Participation as a Human Right,* in Harvard Human Rights Yearbook 77 (1988).

Stewart, Frances, 2005. *Policies towards Horizontal Inequalities in Post-Conflict Reconstruction,* CRISE Working Paper No. 7. March 2005. (CRISE, Queen Elizabeth House, Oxford University).

Tomasevski, Katarina, 1999. *Between Sanctions and Elections. Aid Donors and Their Human Rights Performance.* (London, Pinter).

UNAIDS, Office of the High Commissioner for Human Rights, 2006. *International Guidelines on HIV/AIDS and Human Rights.* Consolidated Version. (Geneva, UNAIDS and OHCHR).

United Nations, Department of Peacekeeping Operations, 2003. *Handbook on UN Multidimensional Peacekeeping Operations.* (New York, United Nations).

United Nations Development Group, 2003. *The Human Rights–Based Approach to Development Cooperation Towards a Common Understanding among UN.* (Stamford, Connecticut.)

United Nations Development Program (UNDP), 1990. *Human Development Report 1990.* (New York, UNDP).

UNDP, 2005. *Governance Indicators. A User's Guide.* 2nd edition. (Oslo, UNDP).

UNDP, 2006. *Indicators for Human Rights Based Approaches to Development. A Users' Guide.*

United Nations. General Assembly, Official Records 62nd session, Supplement No. 53 (A/62/53). *Report of the Human Rights Council A/62/53.* (Geneva).

United Nations, Human Rights Council, 10th Session. January 2009. *Report of the Office of the United Nations High Commissioner for Human Rights on the Relationship between Climate Change and Human Rights.* U.N. Doc. A/HRC/10/61. (Geneva).

United Nations, Human Rights Council, 12th Session, July 30, 2009. *Report of the Working Group on the Right to Development,* on its tenth session (Geneva, June 22–26, 2009). Chairperson-Rapporteur: Arjun Sengupta (India). A/HRC/12/28.

United Nations, Human Rights Council, 15th Session, January 14–22, 2010. *Report of the High Level Task Force on the Implementation of the Right to Development,* on its 6th session. A/HRC/15/WG.2/TF/2/Add.2. (Geneva).

United Nations, Secretary-General, General Assembly, 2005. *In Larger Freedom. Towards Development, Security and Human Rights for All.* A/59/2005. (Geneva).

United Nations. Secretary-General's Report, 1997. *Renewing the United Nations: A Programme for Reform,* UN Doc. A/51/950. (Geneva).

United Republic of Tanzania, Vice President's Office, 2005. *National Strategy for Growth and Reduction of Poverty* (NSGRP). (Dar es Salaam).

Uvin, Peter, 2004. *Human Rights and Development.* (Bloomfield, Kumarian Press).

Vandenhole, Wouter, 2005. *Non-Discrimination and Equality in the View of the UN Human Rights Treaty Bodies.* (Antwerp/Oxford, Intersentia).

VeneKlasen, Lisa Valerie Miller, Cindy Clark, and Molly Reilly, 2004, *Rights-Based Approaches and Beyond: Challenges of Linking Rights and Participation.* In IDS Working Paper No. 235. (Brighton).

Vies, A., 2004. *The Role of Multilateral Development Institutions in Fostering Corporate Social Responsibility,* 47(3) in Development (Inter-American Development Bank). Vol. 47. (Washington, DC).

Workshop Hosted by Irish Aid, organized jointly by the Development Assistance Committee's Networks on Environment and Development, Governance, and Gender Equality and the Working Party on Aid Effectiveness Funded by the Governments of Ireland and Denmark, 2007. *Workshop on Development Effectiveness in Practice. Applying the Paris Declaration to Advancing Gender Equality, Environmental Sustainability and Human Rights.* (OECD, Dublin, April).

World Bank, 1998. *Development and Human Rights: the Role of the World Bank.* (Washington, DC, the World Bank).

World Bank, 1994. *Governance: The World Bank's Experience,* (Washington, DC, the World Bank).

World Bank, 2005. *Empowering People By Transforming Institutions: Social Development in World Bank.* (Washington, DC, The World Bank).

World Bank 2006. *World Development Report 2006. Equity and Development.* (Washington 2006, the World Bank).

World Bank, 2007. *Realizing Rights through Social Guarantees. An Analysis of New Approaches to Social Development.* Report 40047-GBL. (Washington, DC, The World Bank Social Development Department).

Internet Sources

Cingranelli-Richards (CIRI) Human Rights Database.
www.humanrightsdata.com

CRISE
http://www.crise.ox.ac.uk/pubs/workingpaper7.pdf.

Human Rights in EU External Relations:
http://www.consilium.europa.eu/showPage.aspx?id=1634&lang=en. Visited July 2010.

Human Rights Compliance Assessment of the Danish Institute for Human Rights
http://www.humanrightsbusiness.org/.

IFC Human Rights Impact Assessment:
www.guidetohria.org. Visited July 2010.

www.metagora.org.

Metagora. Inventory of Initiatives Aimed at Measuring Human Rights and Democratic Governance. [Online database]. OECD, Paris21, http://www.metagora.org/html/aboutus/about_inventory.html.

International Bank for Reconstruction and Development Articles of Agreement (amended February 16, 1989) available at
http://siteresources.worldbank.org/EXTABOUTUS/Resources/ibrd-articlesofagreement.pdf.

OECD Aid effectiveness, see http://www.oecd.org/document/4/0,3343,en_2649_3236398_45493060_1_1_1_1,00.html.
OECD Glossary. www.oecd.org/dac/evaluation.
http://www.oecd.org/department/0,3355,en_2649_15577209_1_1_1_1_1,00.html.
http://www.oecd.org/dataoecd/11/41/34428351.pdf.

http://www.ohchr.org/Documents/Publications/PovertyStrategiesen.pdf.
http://www.ohchr.org/english/issues/indicators/documents.htm.
http://www2.ohchr.org/english/issues/development/right/high_level_task_force_Right_to_Development.htm.
http://www.unhch.ch/development/approaches-04.html.

http://www.portal-stat.admin.ch/iaos2000/01iaos.htm.

http://www.unglobalcompact.org/AboutTheGC/index.html

Policy of Sweden for Global Development:
http://www.sweden.gov.se/sb/d/3102;jsessionid=aYYdMG4jcq_h.

Political Terror Scale
http://www.politicalterrorscale.org/.

http://www.undp.org/mdg/.
http://www.undp.org/mdg/tracking_targetlist.shtml.

United Nations Statistics. Millennium Development Goals:
http://unstats.un.org/unsd/mdg/Default.aspx. Visited July 2010.

World Bank Comprehensive Development Framework.
http://web.worldbank.org/WBSITE/EXTERNAL/PROJECTS/STRATEGIES/CDF/0,,pagePK:60447~theSitePK:140576,00.html. Visited July 2010.
www.Worldbank.org/cdf.
http://info.worldbank.org/governance/wgi2007/ visited July 2010.
The World Bank Group.
http://ddp-ext.worldbank.org/ext/GMIS/gdmis.do?siteId=2&menuId=LNAV01HOME1. Visited July 2010.
The World Bank, the Nordic Trust Fund.
http://go.worldbank.org/PKPTI6FU40. Visited on 3/29/2010.
http://econ.worldbank.org/WBSITE/EXTERNAL/EXTDEC/EXTRESEARCH/EXTWDRS/EXTWDR2004/0,,menuPK:477704~pagePK:64167702~piPK:64167676~theSitePK:477688,00.html. Visited July 2010.

The Core International Instruments and the Treaty Bodies

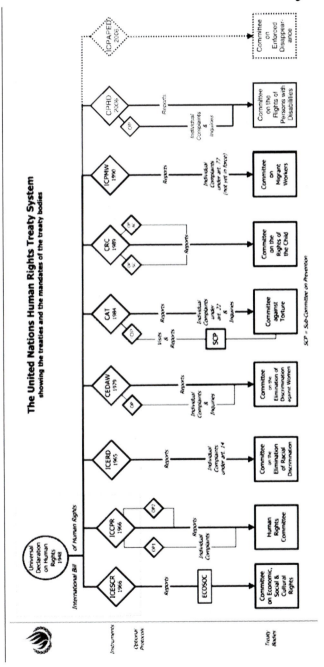

The United Nations Human Rights Treaty System
showing the treaties and the mandates of the treaty bodies

A Structure of Human Rights Indicators

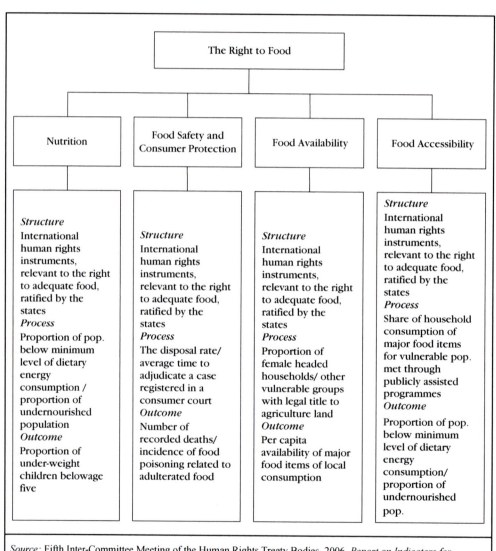

The Right to Food

| Nutrition | Food Safety and Consumer Protection | Food Availability | Food Accessibility |

Nutrition

Structure
International human rights instruments, relevant to the right to adequate food, ratified by the states
Process
Proportion of pop. below minimum level of dietary energy consumption / proportion of undernourished population
Outcome
Proportion of under-weight children belowage five

Food Safety and Consumer Protection

Structure
International human rights instruments, relevant to the right to adequate food, ratified by the states
Process
The disposal rate/ average time to adjudicate a case registered in a consumer court
Outcome
Number of recorded deaths/ incidence of food poisoning related to adulterated food

Food Availability

Structure
International human rights instruments, relevant to the right to adequate food, ratified by the states
Process
Proportion of female headed households/ other vulnerable groups with legal title to agriculture land
Outcome
Per capita availability of major food items of local consumption

Food Accessibility

Structure
International human rights instruments, relevant to the right to adequate food, ratified by the states
Process
Share of household consumption of major food items for vulnerable pop. met through publicly assisted programmes
Outcome
Proportion of pop. below minimum level of dietary energy consumption/ proportion of undernourished pop.

Source: Fifth Inter-Committee Meeting of the Human Rights Treaty Bodies, 2006. *Report on Indicators for Monitoring Compliance with International Human Rights Instruments.* HRI/MC/2006/7. May 11.

Human Rights Indicators Sources

The Cingranelli-Richards (CIRI) Human Rights Database

Purpose	Assessing status of human rights violations of civil and political rights and women's rights
Use	Designed for use by scholars and students to test theories about the causes and consequences of human rights violations, as well as policy makers and analysts who seek to estimate the human rights effects of a wide variety of institutional changes and public policies.
Data sources	U.S. State Department and Amnesty International country reports
Method of data translation	Countries are rated according to the following variables on the basis of quantitative assessment of numbers of violated cases:
	Political or extrajudicial killings; unlawful or arbitrary deprivation of life
	Disappearances
	Torture
	Political imprisonment
	Freedom of speech and press
	Freedom of religion
	Freedom of movement
	Freedom of assembly and association
	Political participation
	Worker rights
	Women's political rights
	Woman's economic rights
	Woman's social rights
Further information	www.humanrightsdata.com

Political Terror Scale

Purpose	Assessing (judgment of human rights conditions)
Use	Used by scholars to examine the relationship between human rights and aid or development
Data sources	U.S. State Department and Amnesty International country reports
Method of data translation	Rating of country reports on a 5-point scale, where 1 signifies that the country is under secure rule of law and 5 signifies that there is a high level of violations of civil and political rights in the country.
Further information	http://www.politicalterrorscale.org/

The CEDAW Assessment Tool (American Bar Association (ABA) and Central European and Eurasian Law Initiative (CEELI))

Purpose	To assess the status of women as reflected in a country's laws and based on the degree to which women in practice the rights and protections guaranteed by CEDAW.
Use	Intended to be a tool for aid organizations and governments to determine where and how there is a need for intervention.
Data sources	Laws of the state and interviews with a selection of at least 30 local people working in the field of women's rights. Possible interviewees include human rights NGOs, women's rights NGOs, government officials and ministries, trade unions, media representatives, law enforcement officials, judges, prosecutors, law professors, bar association members, social workers, and individuals working at women's health clinics and reproductive health organizations.
Method of data translation	Evaluation carried out by assessment team in corporation with local lawyers or other local expert.
	De jure analysis: national legislation is reviewed to determine the status of women as reflected in a country's laws measured by CEDAW standards.
	De facto analysis: to determine the actual realization of CEDAW in real life in the country. Interviews with local experts to collect information on implementation of laws and realization of rights from the viewpoint of those most involved in and affected by a state's compliance with CEDAW.
	Conversion of data into a numerical scale of 5.
Further information	http://www.abanet.org/rol/publications/cedaw_assessment_tool.shtml .

Judicial Reform Index (American Bar Association (ABA) and Central European and Eurasian Law Initiative (CEELI))

Purpose	To assess the process of reforming the judiciaries in emerging democracies
Use	Enable ABA and CEELI, its funders, and the emerging democracies themselves to better target judicial reform programs and monitor progress toward establishing more accountable, effective, and independent judiciaries.
Data sources	Based on interviews with key informants and on relevant available data.
Method of data translation	Assessors are given a series of 30 statements setting forth factors that indicate the development of an accountable, effective, and independent judiciary. The categories incorporated address the quality, education, and diversity of judges; jurisdiction and judicial powers; financial and structural safeguards; accountability and transparency; and issues affecting the efficiency of the judiciary. Each statement is allocated one of three values: positive, neutral, or negative. When the statement strongly corresponds to the reality in a given country, the country is to be given a score of positive for that statement. However, if the statement is not at all representative of the conditions in that country, it is given a negative.
	The 30 statements are based on both subjective and objective criteria and on criteria examined on some fundamental international norms, such as those set out in the U.N. Basic Principles on the Independence of the Judiciary.
Further information	http://www.abanet.org/rol/publications/judicial_reform_index.shtml

Freedom in the World: Freedom House

Purpose	To assess the degree of freedom in 193 countries and 58 territories in the world as part of Freedom House's *"work to advance the worldwide expansion of political and economic freedom."*
Use	Tool to assess state of political rights and civil liberties in the countries of the world.
Data sources	A broad range of sources of information is used in preparing their reports, including foreign and domestic news reports, academic analyses, nongovernmental organizations, think tanks, individual professional contacts, and visits to the region.
	World Population Data Sheet of the Population Reference Bureau. *The World Almanac and Book of Facts*, the *CIA World Factbook*, the BBC, *World Gazetteer*, the Unrepresented Nations and Peoples Organization (UNPO) and World Bank's World Development Indicators.
Method of data translation	Rating of countries on a 7-point scale:
	The ratings process is based on a checklist of 10 political rights questions and 15 civil liberties questions. Raw points are awarded to each of these questions on a scale of 0 to 4, where 0 points represents the smallest degree and 4 points the greatest degree of rights or liberties present. The highest number of points that can be awarded to the political rights checklist is 40 (or a total of up to 4 points for each of the 10 questions). The highest number of points that can be awarded to the civil liberties checklist is 60 (or a total of up to 4 points for each of the 15 questions). The total number of points awarded to the political rights and civil liberties checklists determines the political rights and civil liberties ratings. Each point total corresponds to a rating of 1 through 7, with 1 representing the highest and 7 the lowest level of freedom.
Further information	http://www.freedomhouse.org/template.cfm?page=15

Definition of Right to Water

Right to water and sanitation

Legal standards	The Right to Water is primarily a part of CESCR article 11.1—Right to a Decent Standard of Living—because the Covenant text "including adequate food, clothing and housing" is not intended to be exhaustive.
	The right to water is also part of the following:
	The right to health (CESCR article 12—see GC 14, para 11–12)
	The right to housing and food (CESCR article 11.1—see GC 4, para 8(b))
	The right to life and human dignity (UDHR article 3; CCPR article 6—see GC 15, para 3).
	The right to primary health care (CRC article 24)
	The right to freedom from discrimination against women in rural areas (CEDAW article 14.2).
Core content according to the Committee on ESCR	The right to water is dealt with in General Comment 15 in which the core content is defined as (GC15, para 37):
	"To ensure access to the minimum essential amount of water, that is sufficient and safe for personal and domestic uses to prevent diseases;
	To ensure the right of access to water and water facilities and services on a non-discriminatory basis, especially for disadvantaged or marginalized groups;
	To ensure physical access to water facilities or services that provide sufficient, safe and regular water; that have a sufficient number of water outlets to avoid prohibitive waiting times; and that are at a reasonable distance from the household;
	To ensure personal security is not threatened when having to physically access to water;
	To ensure equitable distribution of all available water facilities and services;
	To adopt and implement a national strategy and plan of action addressing the whole population [. . .]
	To monitor the extent of the realization, or the non-realization, of the right to water;
	To adopt relatively low-cost targeted water programmes to protect vulnerable and marginalized groups;
	To take measures to prevent, treat and control diseases linked to water, in particular ensuring access to adequate sanitation;"
	"Priority in the allocation of water must be given to the right to water for personal and domestic uses. Priority should also be given to the water resources required to prevent starvation and disease, as well as water required to meet the core obligations of each of the Covenant rights" (GC 15, para 6)
	The right to water must be adequate for human dignity, life and health (GC 15, para 11). The following factors always apply to adequacy: *availability*, *quality* and *accessibility* (physical, economic, non-discrimination and information accessibility) (GC 15, para 12).

GC 14 on the Right to Health says that a dimension of the right relates to *quality,* including the need for "safe and potable water, and adequate sanitation" (GC 14, para 12d). The core content of the right to health further includes an obligation "to ensure access to basic shelter, housing and sanitation, and an adequate supply of safe and potable water" (GC 14, 43(c)).

Approaches of scholars

"There is an urgent need for the international community to meet its commitment to the water sector and to begin addressing the world's water problems with renewed vigour. The RBA [rights-based approach] is a tool for emphasising government obligations and for drawing the world's attention to the state of water resources and management encourages this. It also provides a valuable approach to the implementation and management of water services. Experience documented by development practitioners shows that the RBA improves the overall accessibility, efficiency and sustainability of water-related development projects." Emilie Filmer-Wilson, 2005. The Human Rights-Based Approach to Development. The Right to Water. *Netherlands Quarterly of Human Rights*, Vol. 23, 2, p. 240.

Definition of the Right to Education

The Right to Education

Legal standards	The UDHR article 26: "Everyone has the right to education. Education shall be free, at least in the elementary and fundamental stages. Elementary education shall be compulsory [. . .]"

The CESCR, article 13 and 14 clearly acknowledge "the right of everyone to education" and the obligation to provide primary education "compulsory and available free to all"—or to at least fix a detailed national strategy that ensures that such education is progressively implemented "within a reasonable number of years."

The UNESCO Convention Against Discrimination in Education also affirms the right to education, including the right to free and compulsory primary education that must be provided on a nondiscriminatory basis.

References to the right to education are also included in the following:

CEDAW, article 10 and 16.

CRC article 28 and 29.

The International Convention on the Protection of the Rights of All Migrant Workers and the Members of their Families article 12, 30, 43, and 45. |
| **Core content according to the Committee on ESCR** | The right to education is dealt with in General Comments 11 and 13.

The right to education is framed according to "the four A's" (GC 13, para 6):

Availability: the quantity of institutions and programs. It also concerns the requirements in terms of buildings, sanitation, trained teacher, etc., which are all context-dependent.

Accessibility: has three dimensions: (1) Nondiscrimination; (2) Physical accessibility; and (3) Economic accessibility, underlining the need for education to be affordable to all and, at least, primary education to be free.

Acceptability: cultural adequacy and the acceptability of the form, substance, and methods of the education to students (and parents). Minimum educational standards may be approved by the state.

Adaptability: the education must adapt to the particular needs of the communities and the students.

The core content includes an obligation for the state on the following five points (GC13, para 57):

"Ensure the right of access to public educational institutions and programmes on a non-discriminatory basis."

"Ensure that education conforms to the objectives set out in article 13(1)."

"Provide primary education for all in accordance with article 13(2)(a)," i.e., ensure free and compulsory universal primary education that guarantees to satisfy all children's basic learning needs and are cultural and locally adequate.

"Adopt and implement a national educational strategy which includes provision for secondary, higher and fundamental education." |

"Ensure free choice of education without interference from the State or third parties, subject to conformity with "minimum educational standards" (art. 13(3) and (4))." This entails freedom of parents to choose an education for their children, which is in compliance with their own beliefs and freedom of parents to choose other than public schools.

Transparency is specifically required in relation to an effective monitoring system of the educational system in terms of objectives, progress, and minimum educational standards. As with all the other human rights, the state must also provide an accessible, affordable, timely, and effective system of remedy and redress.

Approaches of international agencies

OHCHR formulates some key elements of the right in relation to poverty reduction and the MDGs and develops indicators for each of these targets. On top of nondiscrimination and free primary education to all, these key indicators focus on eradication of illiteracy and free secondary education to all.

UNESCO employs a rights-based approach to their activities and, as OHCHR, links education with the eradication of poverty. However, the monitoring activities focus on the outcome, irrespective of whether this can be attributed to the implementation of a state obligation with regard to the right to education or not.

Approaches of scholars

Tomaševski developed the 4A scheme and the definition of the core content, as applied by the Committee ESCR. She puts particular emphasis on the right to education of vulnerable groups and stresses the need for remedies for ensuring accountability. She has worked extensively with the issue of indicators for the right.

Coomans focuses on nondiscriminatory access to education, free and compulsory education, special facilities for persons with an educational deficit, quality of education, free choice of education and the right to be educated in the language of one's own choice as the most important elements of the right.

Hunt has also worked on the issue of indicators for the right to education. He stresses the need for establishing the extent of states' obligations and proposes a three-tier set of obligations: (1) obligations applying uniformly to all states (such as the principle of nondiscrimination; (2) a minimum core content of the right to education; and (3) the variable dimension.

Definition of the Right to Social Security

The Right to Social Security

Legal standards	The UDHR, article 25 (1) "Everyone has the right to [. . .] medical care and necessary social services, and the right to security in the event of unemployment, sickness, disability, widowhood, old age or other lack of livelihood in circumstances beyond his control" and (2) "motherhood and childhood are entitled to special care and assistance."
	The CESCR, article 9: "The State Parties to the present Covenant recognize the right of everyone to social security, including social insurance"
	Furthermore, CESCR article 10 requires that: (1) "The widest possible protection and assistance should be accorded to the family"; (2) "Special protection should be accorded to mothers during a reasonable period before and after childbirth. During such period working mothers should be accorded paid leave or leave with adequate social security benefits," (3) "Special measures of protection and assistance should be taken on behalf of all children and young persons without any discrimination for reasons of parentage or other conditions"
	ILO Convention 102 on Social Security (Minimum Standards) creates obligations for benefits with regard to: 1) medical care, 2) cash sickness, 3) maternity, 4) old-age, 5) invalidity, 6) survivors, 7) employment injury, 8) unemployment, 9) family benefits.
	The right to Social Security can also be seen as a part of:
	The right to life (UDHR article 3, CCPR article 6)
	The right to work (CESCR article 6 and 7)
	The right to food (which again is a part of the right to a decent standard of living, CESCR article 11.1)
	The right to health (CESCR article 12 (2d))
	The right to freedom from discrimination against women in the field of employment (CEDAW article 11)
	The right to freedom from discrimination against women in rural areas (CEDAW Art. 14).
Core content according to the Committee on ESCR	During 2006 a draft General Comment no. 20 on the Right to Social Security was elaborated. The draft guidelines define core obligations which are to be implemented with immediate effect; they stress *inter alia* the obligation to ensure access to the minimum essential level of social security that is essential for acquiring water and sanitation, foodstuffs, essential primary health care and basic shelter and housing, and the most basic forms of education. In the revised General guidelines regarding the form and contents of reports to be submitted by states parties to the Committee on ESCR, information required for reporting on article 9 includes the elements included in ILO Convention 102 (see above).
	As all other human rights, the rights must be applied in a non-discriminatory way with due priority to the most vulnerable groups.

Approaches of international agencies	The OHCHR links the right to the concept of social safety nets.
	The ILO outlines a human right to *social protection* which should guarantee access to essential goods and services; promote active socio-economic security and advance individual and social potentials for poverty reduction and sustainable development.
	The World Bank's operates with *social risk management*, which overlaps with the ILO approach to social protection, but social risk management does not provide a normative framework.
Approaches of scholars	Lamarche concludes that risks related to health care, sickness benefits, survivor's benefits and maternity benefits should be part of a priority basket of protected risks.
	Liebenberg links the right to social security to the obligations entailed in the ILO Convention 102 and argues that the right to social assistance is part of the right to an adequate standard of living (article 11). The minimum core obligation should include ensuring that the most disadvantaged and vulnerable groups are provided with basic levels of social security.

Implementation of the Right to Development: Attributes Criteria, Subcriteria, and Indicators

The right to development is the right of peoples and individuals to the constant improvement of their well-being and to a national and global enabling environment conducive to just, equitable, participatory, and human-centred development respectful of all human rights. The attributes, criteria, subcriteria, and indicators listed in the following table are designed to assess the extent to which states are individually and collectively taking steps to establish, promote, and sustain national and international arrangements that create an enabling environment for the realization of the right to development. The responsibility for the creation of this enabling environment encompasses three main levels: (1) states acting collectively in global and regional partnerships;[1] (2) states acting individually as they adopt and implement policies that affect persons not strictly within their jurisdiction;[2] and (3) states acting individually as they formulate national development policies and programs affecting persons within their jurisdiction.[3] In order to assess progress in meeting these responsibilities, a selection of indicators is also listed (for their technical definition and sources, see endnotes).

Attribute 1: Comprehensive and Human-Centered Development Policy

Criteria	Subcriteria	Indicators
1 (a) To promote constant improvement in socioeconomic well-being[4]	1 (a) (i) Health	Public expenditures on primary health;[5] life expectancy at birth;[6] access to essential drugs;[7] low birthweight babies;[8] child mortality;[9] HIV prevalence;[10] births attended by skilled personnel[11]
	1 (a) (ii) Education	Public spending on primary education;[12] school enrolment rates;[13] school completion rates;[14] international scores for student achievement[15]
	1 (a) (iii) Housing and water	Public expenditure on public service provision;[16] access to improved drinking water and sanitation;[17] homelessness rate;[18] cost of housing relative to income;[19] slum populations[20]
	1 (a) (iv) Work and social security	Long-term unemployment;[21] involuntary part-time employment;[22] public expenditure on social security;[23] income poverty rates below national and international lines[24]
	1 (a) (v) Food security and nutrition	Child stunting rates[25]

66

Criteria	Subcriteria	Indicators
1 (b) To maintain stable national and global economic and financial systems[26]	1 (b) (i) Reducing risks of domestic financial crises	National regulatory framework;[27] domestic price stability;[28] stability of investments[29]
	1 (b) (ii) Providing against volatility of national commodity prices	National food price volatility;[30] mechanisms for mediating price swings for food staples;[31] food production volatility;[32] agricultural share in total investment[33]
	1 (b) (iii) Reducing risks of external macroimbalances	Debt sustainability;[34] foreign exchange reserves[35]
	1 (b) (iv) Reducing and mitigating impacts of international financial and economic crises	International macroeconomic policy coordination;[36] counter-cyclical financial flows;[37] stability of private capital flows;[38] policies to avert adverse impact of domestic macro policies on other countries[39]
	1 (b) (v) Protect against volatility of international commodity prices	International commodity prices for food staples;[40] international price stabilization mechanisms;[41] non-agricultural commodity prices[42]
1 (c) To adopt national and international policy strategies supportive of the right to development[43]	1 (c) (i) Right to development priorities reflected in national development plans and programmes	Availability of disaggregated socioeconomic data as element of right to development content in key national development strategy documents[44]
	1 (c) (ii) Right to development priorities reflected in policies and programs of IMF, World Bank, WTO, and other international institutions	Equity, nondiscrimination, and right to development objectives in IMF, World Bank, and WTO programs and policies[45]
1 (d) To establish an economic regulatory and oversight system to manage risk and encourage competition[46]	1 (d) (i) System of property rights and contract enforcement	Rule of law governance measures[47]
	1 (d) (ii)Policies and regulations promoting private investment	Regulatory quality governance measures[48]
1 (e) To create an equitable, rule-based, predictable and nondiscriminatory international trading system[49]	1 (e) (i) Bilateral, regional and multilateral trade rules conducive to the right to development	Human rights impact assessment of trade agreements[50] aid for trade[51]
	1 (e) (ii) Market access (share of global trade)	Agricultural export subsidies that adversely affect low-income countries;[52] agricultural imports from developing countries;[53] tariffs on manufactured goods;[54] tariffs on developing-country exports;[55] tariff peaks;[56] manufactured exports[57]
	1 (e) (iii) Movement of persons	Ratification of the International Convention on the Protection of the Rights of All Migrant Workers and Members of Their Families[58]

(continued)

Attribute 1: Comprehensive and Human-Centered Development Policy (continued)

Criteria	Subcriteria	Indicators
1 (f) To promote and ensure access to adequate financial resources[59]	1 (f) (i) Domestic resource mobilization	Effective taxation policies that ensure mobilization of maximum available resources for fulfilment of human rights[60]
	1 (f) (ii) Magnitude and terms of bilateral official capital flows	Net ODA flows relative to donor national incomes with 0.7 percent MDG benchmark and recipient national incomes;[61] program-based aid;[62] quality of aid[63]
	1 (f) (iii) Magnitude and terms of multilateral official capital flows	Proposals for innovative sources for financing international development[64]
	1 (f) (iv) Debt sustainability	External debt relative to exports[65]
1 (g) To promote and ensure access to the benefits of science and technology[66]	1 (g) (i) Pro-poor technology development strategy	Existence of policy framework for technology development targeted at poor people's needs[67]
	1 (g) (ii) Agricultural technology	Improvement in agricultural technology;[68] aid allocation to agriculture[69]
	1 (g) (iii) Manufacturing technology	Technology component of exports;[70] performance requirement provisions in trade agreements[71]
	1 (g) (iv) Technology transfer, access and national capacity	Electricity consumption;[72] Internet coverage;[73] intellectual property and licensing,[74] intellectual property and technology transfer provisions in trade agreements[75]
	1 (g) (v) Green energy technology	Development cooperation for green technologies;[76] use of TRIPS flexibilities to acquire green technologies[77]
	1 (g) (vi) Health technology	Aid allocations to health technologies;[78] use of TRIPS flexibilities and price discounts to expand access to HIV antiretroviral drugs[79]
	1 (g) (vii) Information technology	Access to telecommunications infrastructure[80]
1 (h) To promote and ensure environmental sustainability and sustainable use of natural resources[81]	1 (h) (i) Prevent environmental degradation and resource depletion	Ratification of environmental conventions;[82] consumption of ozone-depleting substances;[83] fishing subsidies;[84] tropical timber imports;[85] gasoline taxes[86]
	1 (h) (ii) Access to natural resources	Value of natural capital;[87] consultative process for respecting the rights of indigenous peoples over natural resources[88]
	1 (h) (iii) Sustainable energy policies and practices	Renewable energy supply[89]
1 (i) To contribute to an environment of peace and security[90]	1 (i) (i) Reduce conflict risks	Transparency in extractive resources trade;[91] socioeconomic disparities between ethnic and other groups;[92] adoption of international arms control measures;[93] implementation of international schemes to restrict marketing of natural resources that fuel conflicts[94] Index[95]

Criteria	Subcriteria	Indicators
	1 (i) (ii) Protecting the vulnerable during conflict	Civilian deaths and internally displaced during conflict;[96] commitment to participation of women in peace processes[97]
	1 (i) (iii) Post-conflict peace building and development	Mechanisms for transitional justice;[98] aid allocations for disarmament;[99] rehabilitation and integration directed specifically at vulnerable groups[100]
	1 (i) (iv)Refugees and asylum-seekers	Contribution to hosting refugees[101]
	1 (i) (v) Personal security not in times and zones of armed conflict	Homicide rates[102] (preferably disaggregated); political stability and absence of violence[103]
1 (j) To adopt and periodically review national development strategies and plans of action on the basis of a participatory and transparent process[104]	1 (j) (i) Collection and public access to key socioeconomic data disaggregated by population groups	Disaggregated socioeconomic indicators[105]
	1 (j) (ii) Plan of action with monitoring and evaluation systems	Existence of systems[106]
	1 (j) (iii) Political and financial support for participatory process	See the following attribute 2 list

Attribute 2: Participatory Human Rights Processes

Criteria	Subcriteria	Indicators
2 (a) To establish a legal framework supportive of sustainable human-centered development[107]	2 (a) (i) Ratification of relevant international conventions	Ratification of the International Covenant on Economic, Social and Cultural Rights, the International Covenant on Civil and Political Rights, the Convention on the Rights of the Child and conventions relating to environment,[108] disadvantaged and marginalized populations,[109] and labor standards[110]
	2 (a) (ii) Responsiveness to international monitoring and review procedures	State reporting, acting upon findings and recommendations and views of treaty bodies and cooperation with special procedures and the universal periodic review process[111]
	2 (a) (iii) National legal protection of human rights	Constitutional and legislative guarantees;[112] national human rights institutions protecting human rights[113]
2 (b) To draw on relevant international human rights instruments in elaborating development strategies[114]	2 (b) (i) Human rights–based approach in national development strategies	Human rights in national development plans and PRSPs;[115] responsibility for extraterritorial infringement of human rights, including by business enterprises[116]

(continued)

Attribute 2: Participatory Human Rights Processes (continued)

Criteria	Subcriteria	Indicators
	2 (b) (ii) Human rights–based approach in policy of bilateral and multilateral institutions and agencies	Institutional policy on human rights;[117] human rights impact assessments of WTO agreements and IMF and World Bank programs[118]
2 (c) To ensure nondiscrimination, access to information, participation, and effective remedies[119]	2 (c) (i) Establishment of a framework providing remedies for violations	Percentage of core human rights for which there are constitutional or legal protections and adjudicatory mechanisms;[120] existence of legal protections for human rights defenders[121]
	2 (c) (ii) Establishment of a framework to facilitate participation	Provision of sufficient political and financial support to ensure effective participation of the population in all phases of the development policy and program design, implementation, monitoring, and evaluation;[122] percentage of national and subnational ministries and other public service providers with published procedures to support public participation in the different stages of assessment, planning, implementation, and evaluation of programs and policies;[123] existence of a legal or administrative standard requiring free, informed, prior consent by indigenous communities to the exploitation of natural resources on their traditional lands[124]
	2 (c) (iii) Procedures facilitating participation in social and economic decision making	Freedom of assembly and association;[125] freedom of speech;[126] voice of rights-holders, accountability of duty-bearers[127]
	2 (c) (iv) Establishment of a legal framework supportive of nondiscrimination	Percentage of core human rights for which there are constitutional or legal protections specifically for women;[128] percentage of core human rights for which there are constitutional or legal protections ensuring equal rights for citizens regardless of race or ethnicity[129]
	2 (c) (v) Establishment of assessment and evaluation system supportive of nondiscrimination	Percentage of sectoral ministries that can provide all of the following for each of its core programs and projects: assessment of relevant vulnerable groups in the context of the program or project, including groups that are vulnerable to discrimination and groups that are vulnerable for other reasons;[130] baseline assessment data of the current state of access to relevant services disaggregated to reflect relevant vulnerable groups;[131] monitoring systems for the program or policy that provide disaggregated information about relevant vulnerable groups[132]

Criteria	Subcriteria	Indicators
	2 (c) (vi) Indicators reflecting likelihood of differential treatment of marginalized groups	Ratio of socioeconomic indicators for marginalized groups to the national average;[133] ratio of percentage of population with advanced HIV infection with access to antiretroviral drugs for marginalized groups to the national average—tracks Millennium Development Goal indicator 6.5;[134] share of the population of marginalized groups incarcerated relative to their share in the population[135]
	2 (c) (vii) Mechanisms for transparency and accountability	Percentage of providers of core public services, whether public or private, for which there exist functional administrative or judicial means of complaint and remedy if standards are violated[136]
2 (d) To promote good governance at the international level and effective participation of all countries in international decision making[137]	2 (d) (i) Mechanisms for incorporating aid recipients' voice in aid programming and evaluation	Percentage of donor support provided through nationally defined coordinated programs: Paris Declaration indicator 4[138]
	2 (d) (ii) Genuine participation of all concerned in international consultation and decision making	IMF voting shares compared to share in global trade;[139] representatives for country participating in negotiations[140]
2 (e) To promote good governance and respect for rule of law at the national level[141]	2 (e) (i) Government effectiveness	Government effectiveness measures[142]
	2 (e) (ii) Control of corruption	Corruption control measures[143]
	2 (e) (iii) Rule of law	Rule of law measures[144]

Attribute 3: Social Justice in Development

Criteria	Subcriteria	Indicators
3 (a) To provide for fair access to and sharing of the benefits of development[145]	3 (a) (i) Equality of opportunity in education, health, housing, employment, and incomes	Income inequality;[146]disaggregated outcome data by population groups, for example, male-female, rural-urban, ethnic-racial, and social-economic status (see indicators for 2 (c) (vi))[147]
	3 (a) (ii) Equality of access to resources and public goods	Public expenditures benefiting poor households[148]
	3 (a) (iii) Reducing marginalization of least developed and vulnerable countries	Global gaps in income and human well-being;[149] mitigating differential bargaining power and adjustment costs of trade liberalization[150]

(continued)

Attribute 3: Social Justice in Development (continued)

Criteria	Subcriteria	Indicators
	3 (a) (iv) Ease of immigration for education, work, and revenue transfers	Flow of skilled and unskilled migrants from poor to rich countries;[151] flow of remittances[152]
3 (b) To provide for fair sharing of the burdens of development[153]	3 (b) (i) Equitably sharing environmental burdens of development	Availability of climate change funds for developing countries;[154] multilateral agreements to reduce negative environmental impacts;[155] distribution of contributions to climate change[156]
	3 (b) (ii) Just compensation for negative impacts of development investments and policies	Hazardous industries, dams, natural resource concessions[157]
	3 (b) (iii) Establishing safety nets to provide for the needs of vulnerable populations in times of natural, financial, or other crisis	Domestic emergency response funds;[158] international humanitarian and reconstruction aid;[159] counter-cyclical official financial flows[160]
3 (c) To eradicate social injustices through economic and social reforms[161]	3 (c) (i) Policies aimed at decent work, which provide for work that is productive and delivers a fair income, security in the workplace, and social protection for families	Growth rate per GDP of person employed, employment to population ratio, proportion of people living on less than a dollar a day[162]
	3 (c) (ii) Elimination of sexual exploitation and human trafficking	Ratification of the protocol to prevent, suppress, and punish trafficking in persons, especially women and children[163]
	3 (c) (iii) Elimination of child labor	Extent of child labor;[164] ratification of the convention on the worst forms of child labor[165]
	3 (c) (iv) Eliminate slum housing conditions	Proportion of urban population living in slums;[166] access to improved sanitation;[167] and secure tenure
	3 (c) (v) Land reform	Access to land;[168] secure land rights;[169] and remedies against land grabs[170]

Notes

[1] See General Assembly resolution 41/128 Declaration on the Right to Development 1986, annex, second preambular paragraph, art. 3.

[2] *Ibid.*, art. 4.

[3] *Ibid.*, art. 2.

[4] *Ibid.*, second preambular paragraph and art. 2.3.

[5] Public expenditures on primary health care as percentage of GDP. Source: World Bank, World Development Indicators Online.

[6] Life expectancy at birth, total. Source: World Bank, World Development Indicators Online.

[7] Proportion of population with access to affordable essential drugs on a sustainable basis (Millennium Development Goal indicator 8.13). Source: http://mdgs.un.org/unsd/mdg/Data.aspx?cr=4.

[8] Percentage of low birthweight babies. Source: World Bank, World Development Indicators Online.

[9] Under-five mortality rate (Millennium Development Goal indicator 4.1). Source: World Bank, World Development Indicators Online.

[10] HIV prevalence among population aged 15 to 24 years (Millennium Development Goal indicator 6.1). Source: http://mdgs.un.org/unsd/mdg/Data.aspx?cr=4.

[11] Percentage of births attended by skilled personnel (Millennium Development Goal indicator 5.2). Source: World Bank, World Development Indicators Online.

[12] Public expenditures on primary education as percentage of GNI. Source: World Bank, World Development Indicators Online.

[13] Percentage of 17- to 22-year-olds with fewer than four years of education, Deprivation and Marginalization in Education data set, http://www.unesco.org/fileadmin/MULTIMEDIA/HQ/ED/GMR/html/dme-3.html. Net secondary school enrolment rate. Source: World Bank, World Development Indicators Online.

[14] Percentage of pupils starting in grade one who will reach last grade of primary school (Millennium Development Goal indicator 2.2). Source: http://mdgs.un.org/unsd/mdg/Data.aspx?cr=4.

[15] Average score on the Programme for International Student Assessment. Source: OECD Program for International Student Assessment, available from http://www.oecd.org/pages/0,3417,en_32252351_32236130_1_1_1_1_1,00.html.

[16] Public expenditure on electricity or other forms of clean energy, water supply, sanitation, and road infrastructure as percentage of GNI. Source: national estimates.

[17] Percentage of population with access to improved drinking water (Millennium Development Goal 7.8) and percentage of population with access to improved sanitation (Goal 7.9). Source: http://mdgs.un.org/unsd/mdg/Data.aspx?cr=4.

[18] Percentage of population homeless. Source: national data (no international data sets available).

[19] Percentage of renters spending more than 30 percent of household income on housing. Source: national data (no international data sets available).

[20] Percentage of urban population living in slums (Millennium Development Goal indicator 7.10). Source: http://mdgs.un.org/unsd/mdg/Data.aspx?cr=4MDG indicators database.

[21] Percentage of labor force unemployed. Source: ILO, KILM database http://www.ilo.org/empelm/what/pubs/lang--en/WCMS_114060/index.htm.

[22] Percentage of labor force working part-time involuntarily. Source: ILO, KILM database (www.ilo.org/empelm/what/pubs/lang--en/WCMS_114060/index.htm).

[23] Public expenditure on social security as percentage of GNI. Source: national statistical services.

[24] For high-income countries, percentage of population with less than 50 percent of median income. Source: Luxembourg Income Study Dataset for developing countries: percentage of population living on less than $1.25 (2005 purchasing power parity per day) (Millennium Development Goal 1.1). Source: http://mdgs.un.org/unsd/mdg/Data.aspx?cr=4.

[25] Prevalence of underweight children under 5 years of age (Millennium Development Goal 1.8). Source: http://mdgs.un.org/unsd/mdg/Data.aspx?cr=4.

[26] *Ibid.*, 14th and 15th preambular paragraphs and arts. 2.2, 2.3, 3.1, 3.3, and 10.

[27] Existence of a transparent, banking regulatory framework and supervisory system sufficient to ensure the integrity of monetary and banking system, mitigate systemic risk, protect consumers and investors, and ensure fairness and efficiency of markets. Source: national policy documents (no international data sets available).

[28] Inflation rate (GDP deflator) below 20 percent. Source: World Bank, World Development Indicators Online.

[29] Ratio of current year to average past five years gross domestic capital formation as percentage of GDP. Source: World Bank, World Development Indicators Online.

[30] Ratio of average annual value to average over preceding five years of FAO food price index. Source: FAO, www.fao.org/worldfoodsituation/foodpricesindex/en.

[31] Existence of national system of buffer stocks. Source: national policy documents.

[32] Ratio of current year to average past five years net per capita production. Source: www.fao.org/worldfoodsituation/foodpricesindex/en.

[33] Allocations to agricultural sector in national investment budgets (from domestic and external resources). Source: national budget and plan documents (no data sets available).

[34] Ratio of debt to exports. Ratio of debt to government revenue. Source: World Bank, *Global Development Finance*; debt management software system in place, such as DMFAS or CS-DRMS. Source: national documentation.

[35] Ratio of reserves to short-term debt, and ratio of reserves to average monthly imports. Source: World Bank, *Global Development Finance*.

[36] Percentage of coordinated macropolicy decisions by G-8 and G-20 countries that incorporate their human development impact. Source: records of G-8 and G-20 meetings and background policy documents (no international data sets available).

[37] Year-to-year percentage change in total IMF credit and loans disbursed (net transfer International Bank for Reconstruction and Development and International Development Association loans outstanding, official net transfer) in proportion to percentage change in average GNI growth rate of developing countries. Source: World Bank, *Global Development Finance*.

[38] Ratio of current-year net transfer private non-publicly guaranteed external debt to average over past five-year net transfer. Source: World Bank, *Global Development Finance*.

[39] Existence of national policy guidelines. Source: national government policy documentation.

[40] Ratio of average annual value to average value over preceding five years of FAO food price index. Source: www.fao.org/worldfoodsituation/foodpricesindex/en.

[41] Existence of global or globally coordinated institutions capable of mediating price swings on key staple foods (corn, oilseed, soybean, rice, wheat), e.g., global buffer stock system. Source: www.fao .org/worldfoodsituation/foodpricesindex/en.

[42] Ratio current year to preceding five years of average value price index for non-agricultural raw materials (minerals, ores and metals, crude petroleum). Source: UNCTAD, Commodity Price Bulletin.

[43] *Ibid.*, third preambular paragraph, arts. 2.3, 3.1, 4, and 10. See also the report of the International Conference on Financing for Development (A/CONF.198/11), para. 11.

[44] Existence and accessibility of key socioeconomic indicators disaggregated by population groups, such as region, ethnicity or linguistic affiliation, race, gender, rural and urban location. Source: national statistical data (no international data sets available).

[45] For IMF, World Bank, and WTO: does the institution explicitly take a rights-based approach to its work, with particular attention to equality and nondiscrimination, transparency, participation, and accountability? Source: IMF, World Bank, WTO policy statements (no international data sets available).

[46] See General Assembly resolutions 41/128, 14th preambular paragraph, arts. 2.2, 2.3, and 3.1; 63/303, para. 37; and the Monterrey Consensus (A/CONF.198/11), paras. 20 and 21.

[47] World Bank Worldwide Governance Indicators Project Index for "Rule of Law." Source: http:// info.worldbank.org/governance/wgi/index.asp. In the light of the conceptual and methodological considerations made in the present report, further research is required.

[48] World Bank Worldwide Governance Indicators Project Index for 'Regulatory Quality." Source: http://info.worldbank.org/governance/wgi/index.asp. In the light of the conceptual and methodological considerations made in the present report, further research is required.

[49] See General Assembly resolution 41/128, 15th preambular paragraph, and arts. 3.3 and 4; General Assembly resolution 64/172, 9th preambular paragraph, and para. 26; and Human Rights Council resolution S-10/1, para. 7.

[50] Existence of requirement to conduct prior impact assessment of the complaint remedy sought on human development in the opposing party, as well as domestically. Source: National Government documentation (no international data sets available).

[51] Proportion of ODA allocated to aid for trade objectives. Source: donor agency data (no international data sets available).

[52] Agricultural support estimate as percentage of the value of agricultural output. Source: compute from the World Development Indicators Online, World Bank.

[53] Value of agricultural imports from developing countries (least developed, landlocked, small-island developing, low-income, middle-income) as a percentage of value of agricultural consumption in OECD countries. Source: UNCTAD, Trade Analysis and Information System database (http:// r0.unctad.org/trains_new/index.shtm).

[54] Average tariff rate in OECD countries on manufactured goods originating from least developed, low- and middle-income countries. Source: UNCTAD, Trade Analysis and Information System database (http://r0.unctad.org/trains_new/index.shtm).

[55] Average tariff revenues received from countries with lower per capita income levels. Source: UNCTAD Trade Analysis and Information System database (http://r0.unctad.org/trains_new/index .shtm) and World Bank, World Integrated Trade Solution (http://wits.worldbank.org/witsweb/FAQ/ Basics.aspx).

[56] Number of manufactured products subject to tariff peaks. Source: UNCTAD Trade Analysis and Information System database (http://r0.unctad.org/trains_new/index.shtm); and the World Bank World Integrated Trade Solution (http://wits.worldbank.org/witsweb/FAQ/Basics.aspx).

[57] Value of exports as percentage share of global trade. Source: United Nations Statistics Division Comtrade Database.

[58] Percentage of countries that have ratified the International Convention on the Protection of the Rights of All Migrant Workers and Members of Their Families. Source: treaty body database (www .unhchr.ch/tbs/doc.nsf/Statusfrset?OpenFrameSet).

[59] See General Assembly resolution 41/128, 14th and 15th preambular paragraphs, arts. 4.2 and 8; General Assembly resolution 63/303, paras. 10, 11, and 14; and the Monterrey Consensus (A/ CONF.198/11), para. 15.

[60] Government revenue as percentage of GDP. Source: World Bank, World Development Indicators Online.

[61] Net ODA as percentage of GNI (Millennium Development Goal indicator 8.1). Source: OECD (www.oecd.org/dac/stats/data).

[62] Percentage of aid provided through program-based approaches (Paris Declaration Indicator 9). Source: OECD, 2008 Survey on Monitoring the Paris Declaration: Effective Aid by 2010? What Will It Take, Vol. 1; overview available at (http://siteresources.worldbank.org/ACCRAEXT/Resources/Full -2008-Survey-EN.pdf).

[63] Quality of aid indicator of Commitment to Development Index. Source: Center for Global Development (www.cgdev.org/section/topics/aid_effectiveness). In the light of the conceptual and methodological considerations made in the present report, further research is required.

[64] Number of times that innovative proposals for financing (e.g., Tobin tax, airline tax) feature on the agenda of G-8 and G-20 meetings, and of intergovernmental meetings on financing for development. Source: records of G-8 and G-20 meetings and of U.N. meetings on financing for development.

[65] Ratio of debt to exports. Source: World Bank, Global Development Finance.

[66] See General Assembly resolutions 41/128, 3rd, 10th, and 16th preambular paragraphs, arts. 2.3, 3.3, and 4; 55/2, para. 20; and 60/1, para. 60.

[67] Existence of national policy statement on science in technology. Source: national development plan or other strategy document (such as poverty reduction strategy paper). Source: national Government documentation (no international data sets available).

[68] Trends yields of main staple crops (rice, wheat, corn, cassava, plantain). Source: FAO statistics (http://faostat.fao.org/default.aspx).

[69] Share of ODA dedicated to agricultural sector development. Source: OECD aid statistics (www .oecd.org/dataoecd/50/17/5037721.htm).

[70] High technology exports as percentage of total exports of goods. Source: U.N. Statistical Division Comtrade.

[71] Percentage of bilateral and regional trade agreements that prohibit developing countries from using performance criteria (such as local content requirements, technology transfer requirements, and local employment requirements) to maximize benefits of foreign direct investment on national development. Source: content review of bilateral and regional trade agreements (no international data sets available).

[72] Kilowatt hours per capita. Source: World Bank, World Development Indicators Online.

[73] Internet hosts per 1,000 people. Source: International Telecommunications Union, World Internet Reports.

[74] Patents granted to residents. Source: WIPO Intellectual Property Statistics.

[75] Bilateral trade agreements and regional trade agreements that include conditions tightening intellectual property rights protection beyond the agreed levels of the TRIPS Agreement. Source: review of bilateral and regional trade agreements.

[76] Share of ODA devoted to promoting green technologies. Source: OECD (www.oecd.org/dataoecd/ 50/17/5037721.htm).

[77] Number of cases. Source: national Government documentation (no international data sets available).

[78] Share of ODA dedicated to health technologies. Source: OECD aid statistics (www.oecd.org/ dataoecd/50/17/5037721.htm).

[79] Proportion of population with advanced HIV infection receiving antiretroviral therapy (Millennium Development Goal target 6.B). Source: Millennium Development Goals database (http://unstats.un.org/unsd/mdg/Default.aspx).

[80] Mainline and cellular telephones per 1,000 people (Millennium Development Goal target 8.F). Source: Millennium Development Goals database (http://unstats.un.org/unsd/mdg/Default.aspx).

[81] See General Assembly resolution 41/128, arts. 1.2 and 3.1; General Assembly resolution 60/1, para. 10; and the Monterrey Consensus (A/CONF.198/11), paras. 3 and 23.

[82] Ratification of key environmental conventions. Source: OHCHR treaty body database (www.unhchr.ch/tbs/doc.nsf/Statusfrset?OpenFrameSet).

[83] CO_2 emissions, kg per \$1,000 (PPP) of GDP; CO_2 emissions per capita. Source: World Bank, World Development Indicators Online.

[84] Fishing subsidies per capita. Source: OECD, Review of Fisheries in OECD Countries, Policies and Summary Statistics, 2005.

[85] Value of tropical timber imports per capita. Source: national statistics (no international data sets available).

[86] No data source identified to date.

[87] Value of natural capital. Source: World Bank environmental indicators (http://web.worldbank.org/ WBSITE/EXTERNAL/TOPICS/ENVIRONMENT/EXTEEI/0,,contentMDK:21005068~pagePK:210058 ~piPK:210062~theSitePK:408050,00.html).

[88] Existence of requirement for consultation process in regulations governing foreign direct investment. Source: national documentation (no international data sets available).

[89] Clean energy production as percentage of total energy supply. Source: World Bank, World Development Indicators Online.

[90] See General Assembly resolutions 41/128, 9th, 11th, and 12th preambular paragraphs, arts. 3.2 and 7; and 60/1, paras. 5, 69–118.

[91] Existence of national standards requiring transparency in payment arrangements to governments (home or host country) by businesses engaged in extractive industries vulnerable to capture by parties to violent conflict. Source: national legislation.

[92] Measures of horizontal inequality or disparities between identity groups in the country: ratio of ethnic group to national average values for key socioeconomic indicators. Source: calculations based on national data disaggregated by ethnic group.

[93] Participation in one or more international agreements or standards regulating trade in small arms (Wassenaar Arrangement on Export Controls for Conventional Arms and Dual-Use Goods and Technologies). Source: Wassenaar Arrangement (www.wassenaar.org).

[94] Country commitment to Kimberley Process. Source: Kimberley Process Working Group.

[95] Security index in Commitment to Development Index. Source: Center for Global Development (www.cgdev.org/section/topics/aid_effectiveness). In the light of the conceptual and methodological considerations made in the present report, further research is required.

[96] Annual number of civilian deaths per 100,000 population during years of and year following armed conflict. Source: UCDP/PRIO armed conflict data.

[97] Adoption of a national plan of action in accordance with Security Council resolution 1325 (2000) on women and peace and security. Source: national sources (no international database available).

[98] Existence of mechanisms for transitional justice within five years of cessation of hostilities. Source: national documentation (no international data sets).

[99] Proportion of aid allocations for disarmament. Source: OECD aid statistics (www.oecd.org/ dataoecd/50/17/5037721.htm).

[100] Proportion of ODA for disarmament, rehabilitation, and reintegration targeted at issues affecting women. Source: OECD aid statistics (www.oecd.org/dataoecd/50/17/5037721.htm).

[101] UNHCR index of refugee burden. Source: UNHCR Statistical Yearbook.

[102] Homicides per 100,000. Source: United Nations Office on Drugs and Crime (www.unodc.org/ unodc/en/data-and-analysis/index.html?ref=menuside).

[103] Political stability and absence of violence index score, worldwide governance indicators. (www .worldbank.org/wbi/governance). In the light of the conceptual and methodological considerations made in the present report, further research is required.

[104] See General Assembly resolution 41/128, second preambular paragraph, arts. 1.1, 2.3, 3.1, and 8.2.

[105] Data on key socioeconomic indicators, disaggregated by major population group, including gender, race, ethnicity, and rural population. Source: national statistical data.

[106] Existence of systems. Source: national Government processes.

[107] *Ibid.*, 5th, 8th, and 13th preambular paragraphs, arts. 1.1, 2.1, and 10.

[108] Ratification. Source: OHCHR treaty body database (www.unhchr.ch/tbs/doc.nsf/ Statusfrset?OpenFrameSet).

[109] Ratification. Source: OHCHR treaty body database (www.unhchr.ch/tbs/doc.nsf/ Statusfrset ?OpenFrameSet).

[110] Ratification. Source: OHCHR treaty body database (www.unhchr.ch/tbs/doc.nsf/ Statusfrset ?OpenFrameSet).

[111] Existence of state reports. Source: OHCHR documentation.

[112] Existence of relevant legislation or administrative instructions. Source: national constitution and legislation.

[113] Existence of national human rights institutions. Source: national government information.

[114] See *Ibid.*, 8th and 10th preambular paragraphs, arts. 3.3, 6, and 9.2; and General Assembly resolution 64/172, para. 9.

[115] Human rights as an element of normative framework, analysis of critical constraints, and priority plan of action. Source: content review of relevant documents.

[116] Existence of national regulation. Source: national government information (no international database available).

[117] Human rights elements of institutional policy statements. Source: review of institutional statements (no data sets available).

[118] Human rights impact assessments of WTO, IMF, and World Bank programmes. Source: studies from diverse origins (no data sets available to date).

[119] See General Assembly resolutions 41/128, second and eighth preambular paragraphs, arts. 1.1, 5, 6, and 8.2; and 64/172, paras. 9 and 29.

[120] Percentage of core human rights for which there are constitutional or legal protections and adjudicatory mechanisms. Source: content review of legal and administrative references (no data sets available).

[121] Existence of legal protection for human rights defenders. Source: content review of legal and administrative references (no data sets available).

[122] Budget provided for participatory processes. Source: country-specific budgets at ministerial level (no data sets available).

[123] Existence of published guidelines in national and subnational ministries and agencies. Source: country-specific administrative information (no data sets available).

[124] Existence of guidelines and procedures. Source: country-specific administrative information (no data sets available).

[125] Further research required.

[126] Further research required.

[127] World Bank Worldwide Governance Indicators Voice and Accountability score. Source: World Bank (http://info.worldbank.org/governance/wgi/index.asp). In the light of the conceptual and methodological considerations made in the present report, further research is required.

[128] Existence of legal provisions. Source: country-specific assessment. Source: no international data sets available.

[129] Existence of legal provisions. Source: country-specific assessment. Source: no international data sets available.

[130] Existence of studies. Source: country-specific assessments (no international data sets available).

[131] Existence of studies. Source: country-specific assessments (no international data sets available).

[132] Existence of studies. Source: country-specific assessments (no international data sets available).

[133] Ratio of value for marginalized population (ethnic group, racial group, women, disabled, aged, other identified groups) to national average for indicators under I (a) including health, education, housing, and water, work and social security, food security and nutrition. Sources: sources identified with regard to attribute 1 (a). Note: Millennium Development Goal monitoring guidelines recommend collection of disaggregated data.

[134] Ratio of value for marginalized population to national average with access to antiretroviral drugs (Millennium Development Goal indicator 6.5). Note: Millennium Development Goal indicators guidelines recommend collection of disaggregated data.

[135] Ratio of incarceration rate for marginalized population to national average. Source: national statistical data (no international data sets available).

[136] Country-specific assessments. Source: no international data sets available.

[137] See General Assembly resolution 41/128, arts. 3 and 10; General Assembly resolution 64/172, para. 10 (a); the Monterrey Consensus (A/CONF.198/11), paras. 7, 38, 53, 57, 62, and 63; and Human Rights Council resolution S-10/1, para. 3.

[138] Percentage of donor support provided through nationally defined programs (Paris Declaration monitoring indicator 4). Source: OECD, 2008 survey on monitoring the Paris Declaration: effective aid by 2010? What Will It take? Vol. 1.

[139] Ratio of percentage IMF quotas to share in global trade. Source: World Bank, World Development Indicators Online and IMF (www.imf.org/external/np/sec/memdir/members.htm).

[140] Ratio country average to high-income country average in average number of WTO representatives per country party to negotiations for multilateral trade agreement. Source: WTO delegations and negotiations records (no data sets available).

[141] General Assembly resolutions 41/128, arts. 1.1, 2.3, 3.1, 6.3, 8.1, and 10; and 64/172, paras. 9, 10 (e), 27, and 28.

[142] Worldwide Governance Indicators Government Effectiveness Index. Source: World Bank Worldwide Governance Indicators (http://info.worldbank.org/governance/wgi/index.asp). In the light of the conceptual and methodological considerations made in the present report, further research is required.

[143] Worldwide Governance Indicators Corruption Index. Source: World Bank Worldwide Governance Indicators (http://info.worldbank.org/governance/wgi/index.asp). In the light of the conceptual and methodological considerations made in the present report, further research is required.

[144] Worldwide Governance Indicators Rule of Law Index. Source: World Bank Worldwide Governance Indicators (http://info.worldbank.org/governance/wgi/index.asp). In the light of the conceptual and methodological considerations made in the present report, further research is required.

[145] General Assembly resolution 41/128, first and second preambular paragraphs, arts. 1.1, 2.3, and 8.

[146] Ratio of income of bottom quintile to bottom quintile population (by country). Source: World Bank, World Development Indicators Online.

[147] Ratio of key socioeconomic outcome data between population groups (rural, female, ethnic group, linguistic group, racial group) and national average. Source: calculation based on disaggregated national data as in subcriteria 2 (c) (vi).

[148] Ratio of combined school enrolment rate of poorest population quintile to wealthiest population quintile; public expenditure on economic infrastructure and services benefiting smallholders and business owners as percentage of GNI; ratio of income growth rate of poorest population quintile to income growth rate of wealthiest population quintile. Source: calculations based on national data (no international data sets available).

[149] Ratio of average per capita GDP growth rate of poorest quintile of countries to average per capita GDP growth rate of wealthiest quintile of countries; ratio of under-five mortality rate average in least developed countries to rate in high-income countries; ratio of net secondary enrolment rate average in least developed countries to global average; ratio of percentage of children under 5 years who are shorter for age average in least developed countries compared to global average. Source: World Bank, World Development Indicators Online.

[150] Proportion of total OECD country imports from least-developed countries admitted free of duty (Millennium Development Goal indicator 8.6). Source: Millennium Development Goal indicators data set.

[151] Foreign nationals of developing countries with valid work permits as percentage of high-income country labor force. Source: national data (no international data sets available).

[152] Inflow of remittances. Source: World Bank, World Development Indicators Online.

[153] See *Ibid.*, arts. 2.2 and 8.1 and Human Rights Council resolution S-10/1, para. 5.

[154] Value of global funds (sum of ODA and private contributions) as percentage of global GNI made available to developing countries for activities mitigating the effects of climate change. Source: OECD aid statistics (www.oecd.org/dataoecd/50/17/5037721.htm).

[155] Percentage signed of major environmental treaties (e.g., Cartagena Protocol, Framework Convention on Climate Change, Kyoto Protocol to the Framework Convention, Vienna Convention for the Protection of the Ozone Layer, Montreal Protocol on Substances that Deplete the Ozone Layer, Stockholm Convention on Persistent Organic Pollutants, Convention on the Law of the Sea, Convention to Combat Desertification). Source: documentation on each treaty.

[156] Ratio of per capita CO_2 emissions of high-income countries to those of developing countries (least-developed, landlocked, small-island developing states, low-income, middle-income countries). Source: World Bank, World Development Indicators Online.

[157] Value of compensation per capita for negative impact of development. Source: case specific information (no international data sets available).

[158] Emergency response funds. Source: national budgets (no international data sets).

[159] Humanitarian and reconstruction aid flows as a proportion of appeals. Source: calculation based on case-specific appeal documentation and OECD aid statistics (www.oecd.org/dataoecd/50/17/5037721.htm).

[160] Year-to-year percentage change in total IMF credit and loans disbursed (net transfer IBD and IDA loans outstanding, official net transfer) in proportion to percentage change in GNI growth rate. Source: data from World Bank, *World Development Indicators and Global Development Finance*.

[161] See General Assembly resolution 41/128, art. 8; and the Monterrey Consensus (A/CONF.198/11), para. 16.

[162] These are Millennium Development Goal 1 indicators. Source: Millennium Development Goal indicators data sets (http://mdgs.un.org/unsd/mdg/Default.aspx).

[163] Ratification of the Protocol to Prevent, Suppress and Punish Trafficking in Persons, Especially Women and Children, supplementing the United Nations Convention against Transnational Organized Crime. Source: OHCHR treaty body database (www.unhchr.ch/tbs/doc.nsf Statusfrset?OpenFrameSet).

[164] Children involved in economic activity, child labor, and hazardous work. Source: ILO international programme on the elimination of child labor.

[165] Ratification of treaty. Source: OHCHR treaty body database (www.unhchr.ch/tbs/doc.nsf/Statusfrset?OpenFrameSet).

[166] Percentage of urban population living in slums (Millennium Development Goal indicator 7.D). Source: Millennium Development Goal indicators data sets (http://mdgs.un.org/unsd/mdg/Default.aspx).

[167] Percentage of urban population with access to improved sanitation (Millennium Development Goal indicator 7C). Source: Millennium Development Goal indicators data set (http://mdgs.un.org/unsd/mdg/Default.aspx).

[168] Landless agricultural laborers as proportion of rural labor force. Source: national statistical data (no international data sets).

[169] National legislation on land rights. Source: national legislation (no international data sets).

[170] National legislation and procedures. Source: review of national legislation and guidelines (no international indicator sets available).

Eco-Audit

Environmental Benefits Statement

The World Bank is committed to preserving Endangered Forests and natural resources. We print World Bank Working Papers and Country Studies on postconsumer recycled paper, processed chlorine free. The World Bank has formally agreed to follow the recommended standards for paper usage set by Green Press Initiative—a nonprofit program supporting publishers in using fiber that is not sourced from Endangered Forests. For more information, visit www.greenpressinitiative.org.

In 2009, the printing of these books on recycled paper saved the following:

Trees*	Solid Waste	Water	Net Greenhouse Gases	Total Energy
289	8,011	131,944	27,396	92 mil.
*40 feet in height and 6–8 inches in diameter	Pounds	Gallons	Pounds CO_2 Equivalent	BTUs

9 780821 386040